LEADING
THROUGH AN
EQUITY
LENS

A Process for

Advancing

Inclusive

District

Initiatives

KIM WALLACE

Solution Tree | Press

555 North Morton Street
Bloomington, IN 47404
800.733.6786 (toll free) / 812.336.7700
FAX: 812.336.7790

email: info@SolutionTree.com
SolutionTree.com

Visit **go.SolutionTree.com/diversityandequity** to download the free reproducibles in this book.

Printed in the United States of America

Library of Congress Cataloging-in-Publication Data

Names: Wallace, Kim, author.
Title: Leading through an equity lens : a process for advancing inclusive
    district initiatives / Kim Wallace.
Description: Bloomington, IN : Solution Tree Press, 2023. | Includes
    bibliographical references and index.
Identifiers: LCCN 2022059219 (print) | LCCN 2022059220 (ebook) | ISBN
    9781958590119 (paperback) | ISBN 9781958590126 (ebook)
Subjects: LCSH: Educational equalization--United States. | Educational
    change--United States. | Educational leadership--United States. | School
    districts--United States--Administration.
Classification: LCC LC213.2 .W257 2023 (print) | LCC LC213.2 (ebook) |
    DDC 379.2/6--dc23/eng/20230223
LC record available at https://lccn.loc.gov/2022059219
LC ebook record available at https://lccn.loc.gov/2022059220

Solution Tree
Jeffrey C. Jones, CEO
Edmund M. Ackerman, President

Solution Tree Press
President and Publisher: Douglas M. Rife
Associate Publisher: Sarah Payne-Mills
Managing Production Editor: Kendra Slayton
Editorial Director: Todd Brakke
Art Director: Rian Anderson
Copy Chief: Jessi Finn
Production Editor: Gabriella Jones-Monserrate
Content Development Specialist: Amy Rubenstein
Copy Editor: Madonna Evans
Proofreader: Evie Madsen
Text and Cover Designer: Laura Cox
Associate Editor: Sarah Ludwig
Assistant Acquisitions Editor: Elijah Oates

Acknowledgments

Solution Tree Press would like to thank the following reviewers:

Tonya Alexander
English Teacher (NBCT)
Owego Free Academy
Owego, New York

Gina Cherkowski
Education Researcher
Calgary, Alberta, Canada

Doug Crowley
Assistant Principal
DeForest Area High School
DeForest, Wisconsin

Jed Kees
Principal
Onalaska Middle School
Onalaska, Wisconsin

Hedreich Nichols
Author, Educator, Consultant
SmallBites Educational Consulting
Arlington, Texas

Liza A. Talusan
Associate Instructor
University of Massachusetts, Boston
Boston, Massachusetts

Visit **go.SolutionTree.com/diversityandequity** to download the free reproducibles in this book.

Table of Contents

Reproducibles are in italics.

About the Author

 **Kim Wallace, EdD,** started her career in public education in 1994 as a high school English and social studies teacher before going into site and district administration. She previously served as superintendent of one of the twenty largest school districts in California.

In 2020, Dr. Wallace joined the University of California, Berkeley as the associate director of the 21st Century California School Leadership Academy (21CSLA) to contribute to the wider field of support for educational leaders. She also runs her own consulting business, Process Makes Perfect (https://processmakesperfect.org), specializing in leadership, strategic planning, change management, and emerging trends in education.

Dr. Wallace is author of the book *Leading the Launch: A Ten-Stage Process for Successful School District Initiatives*.

She earned a bachelor's degree in history at the University of California, Santa Barbara, a master's degree at the University of California, Los Angeles, and culminated her educational goals with a doctorate in educational leadership from the University of California, Davis.

To book Kim Wallace for professional development, contact pd@SolutionTree.com.

Introduction

Educational equity has been a centuries-long endeavor in the United States, as well as all over the world. The fact is that schools were not originally meant for everyone. They were primarily reserved for the wealthy, White, and able-bodied male. For centuries, schools were designed (even if by de facto means) to preserve, maintain, and sustain socioeconomic class stratification and operate as a gate-keeper to social and professional advancement for the majority of the population (Thattai, 2001). Horace Mann's then-revolutionary conception of the *common school* in the 1830s was a decentralized system intended to educate all children, free of charge, funded by each state (as cited in Kober & Rentner, 2020). As a result, by 1870, 78 percent of U.S. children received a primary education, but by 1910, only 14 percent had completed high school (Kober & Rentner, 2020). In countries with more centralized systems, the pace was even slower until more than a dozen countries surpassed U.S. graduation rates by the early 21st century, including South Korea, the United Kingdom, and Ukraine (Bada, 2020).

Over the course of the mid to late 20th century, in most industrialized nations, people of color, Indigenous peoples, women, individuals with disabilities, linguistic minorities, and other historically disenfranchised and underserved groups began to rightfully breach the walls of the establishment. Many of these advancements came about in fits and starts via local, state, and national legislation, court decisions, grassroots efforts, civil rights actions, and from pioneers and champions of equal access to education. In their brief history of equality of educational opportunity in the United States, Liam Shields, Anne Newman, and Debra Satz (2017) examine how hallmark judicial and legislative actions—such as *Brown v. Board of Education* (1954), Title IV of the Civil Rights Act of 1964, Title IX of the Education Amendments of 1972, and the Equal Educational Opportunities Act of 1974—were enacted to prohibit discrimination against protected groups.

These pivotal decisions, alongside collective civil rights movements throughout the second half of the 20th century, resulted in primary, secondary, and higher education institutions further opening doors to future employment, upward mobility, family stability, and personal development for diverse groups of people. However, opening the doors proved to only shift the balance to a limited degree. Marginalized peoples continued to face additional hurdles, racism, prejudice, and institutionalized discrimination in their classrooms, out on the athletic field, and in extracurricular activities (Robinson, 2021).

While U.S. women eventually surpassed men in college attendance—from 41.2 percent in 1960 to 57.4 percent by 2019 (Hanson, 2022a)—they still earn significantly less after graduating with a bachelor's degree ($57,340) compared to men ($77,220), according to the United States Census Bureau (2022). When breaking down college attendance rates and earnings by race plus sex, people of color, and women of color especially, are still highly disadvantaged and undervalued. Hispanic women earn an average of 55 cents and Black women earn 63 cents on the dollar earned by White men (Hegewisch & Mariano, 2020). According to the 2021 World Economic Forum annual report on global gender gaps, women still earn about 37 percent less than men in similar roles and based on the current trajectory, women are 267.6 years away from gender parity in the area of economic participation and opportunity. Though a mighty endeavor, the push for equal access for all still falls all too short.

Disconcerted yet galvanized by so much educational injustice, in the 1990s, researchers and activists all over the world began to develop new theories of action to advocate for *equity* rather than pursue *equality* (Jurado de Los Santos, Moreno-Guerrero, Marín-Marín, & Soler Costa, 2020). Equality means that everyone receives the same opportunities, rights, or resources from the system; equity, however, recognizes that since different groups of people start with different circumstances, the supports provided should be proportional to need. This shift, however, when oversimplified, began to denote equality as "bad" and equity as "good," when the complexity is so much greater. Professor of education, Meira Levinson, doctoral student at the Harvard Graduate School of Education, Tatiana Geron, and professor of philosophy at the University of Wisconsin–Madison, Harry Brighouse (2022) surmise that, "Most people working in education agree that 'educational equity' is an important aim of schooling. However, the almost universal acknowledgment that equity is a valuable goal can obscure very real differences in what various people mean by 'equity' and how they operationalize it" (p. 1). Is equity about access or outcomes? Is it about opportunities or attainment? Is it about additional resources for disadvantaged families or annihilation of entire systems? It depends on who you ask.

For additional context, Erica L. Green (2023) of *The New York Times* reports the following:

> The Education Department's Office for Civil Rights logged a record number of discrimination complaints in the past year, the latest indicator of how the social and political strife roiling the country is reverberating in the nation's schools. Nearly 19,000 complaints were filed with the office in the past fiscal year—between Oct. 1, 2021, and Sept. 30, 2022—more than double the previous year and breaking the record of 16,000 filed in fiscal year 2016, according to figures provided by the department.

While progress has been and is continuing to be made toward educational equity, it's clearly not time to rest on our laurels and proclaim we're living in a post-racial world, much less one that is free from danger for any other young people in the United States or other countries' educational systems.

The definition of *equity* is nuanced and evolving, yet it's flexible enough to be applied through various means and approaches. It has also become highly politicized and frequently mischaracterized through the churn of the daily news cycle and social media, so it's important to define it plainly. Philip E. Poekert, Sue Swaffield, Ema K. Demir, and Sage A. Wright (2020) assert that *educational equity* will be realized only when:

> Dimensions of privilege and oppression (e.g. race, ethnicity, socioeconomic status, gender, sexual orientation, religion) are *not predictive of or correlated with educational outcomes* [emphasis added], broadly defined, in any significant way, and where *all learners are able to participate fully in quality learning experiences* [emphasis added]. (pp. 541–542)

To orient readers, this will be our operating definition of educational equity for the remainder of this book.

Furthermore, associate professor of integrative studies at George Mason University and founder of EdChange Paul Gorski (2019) cautions leaders to avoid four "racial equity detours" that "create an illusion of progress toward equity while cementing, or even exacerbating, inequity," including:

1. Insisting on meeting privileged adults "where they are," rather than at the more urgent cadence of those without power, thus slowing the pace of equity-centered measures

2. Employing euphemisms such as "poverty" or "culture" in lieu of directly calling out racism when applicable

3. Using language that suggests students and families need to be fixed rather than naming and tackling deficits within the system

4. Cloaking discrimination by superficially celebrating diversity through events like multicultural food fairs or teaching Black history only in February (pp. 57–59)

We need to push beyond the feel-good catchphrases such as "no child left behind," "every student succeeds," and "all children can learn" that mask or misdiagnose inequities. While the intentions behind those phrases may have been good, they become meaningless without authentic action. This book is designed to help leaders incorporate checks and balances to recognize red herrings and sidestep potential pitfalls.

After decades of preeminent scholarship on advancing equity, Gloria Ladson-Billings (2021) observes:

> In the midst of four pandemics—COVID-19, systemic racism, pending economic collapse, and environmental catastrophe—teachers have the challenge of teaching students who are confronting existential uncertainty and precarious futures. . . . these multiple pandemics also provide the education community with a unique opportunity to re-set and revision our work. (pp. 352–353)

This is the hope sustaining us changemakers out there: equity in action. We will follow in the footsteps of those who have walked before us, while laying our own fresh imprints on the ground.

There are many superb resources out there on equity-related topics by academics, trained professionals, and lifelong practitioners. I am not, nor do I pretend to hold company beside any of the preeminent scholars in this complex and vital domain. If you are new to the concept of educational equity, I suggest reading, watching, or listening to those who are experts on the subject, such as Anthony Muhammad, Gloria Ladson-Billings, Tyrone Howard, Beverly Daniel Tatum, Pedro Noguera, and bell hooks, to ground yourself, as I have, in the research base. What I can and do capably offer is a proven process that helps district leaders keep their equity lens wide open and focused on meeting the needs of underserved groups of students by responsibly and responsively infusing new initiatives into their organizations. This book will help school and district leaders ask the right questions, connect the dots between positive intentions and generating change, and implement new initiatives with integrity.

EQUITY-CENTERED INITIATIVES

The Organisation for Economic Co-operation and Development (OECD; 2008) recommends ten steps to reduce school failure, nested under three umbrellas: (1) design, (2) practices, and (3) resourcing. *Design* is intentionally structuring and organizing systems that promote conditions for success; *practices* include culturally responsive instructional strategies that strengthen connections between school and home; and *resourcing* means channeling proportional and requisite resources to students with the greatest needs. All three must act in concert to support the system as a whole.

So, what exactly are equity-centered new initiatives? They can include any project, process, policy, product, or program that may fit one or more of the following descriptions.

- Are new to the K–12 field or have not yet been tried in your school or district and focus on reducing barriers or improving conditions for historically marginalized students

- Currently exist, but may need significant changes to refocus the work toward educational equity

- Include deliberate research-based approaches that benefit specifically identified groups of families, students, or staff

- Require resources above and beyond what may be currently budgeted or planned for but are worth seeking out in the effort to level the playing field

- Constitute an immediate response to emerging needs or changing conditions that lend opportunities for improving equitable conditions

- Are generated from school sites, governing board, business services, human resources, instructional services, or outside entities (government, legal system, community groups) as a call to right a wrong or take social justice action on behalf of a minoritized group

Simply put, *equity-centered initiatives* are just like any new initiatives, except for the persistent focus on reducing inequities and accelerating opportunities for students who have been disadvantaged, disenfranchised, or traditionally segregated from high-quality learning environments.

FROM LEADING THE LAUNCH TO ADVANCING INCLUSIVE DISTRICT INITIATIVES

To get us started, I want to juxtapose the following two oft-repeated quotes.

"Insanity is doing the same thing over and over and expecting different results."
—Albert Einstein (attributed)

"The people who are crazy enough to think they can change the world are the ones who do."
—Steve Jobs

Though it is not professional or advisable to use terms such as *insanity* and *crazy* because they perpetuate the stigma attached to individuals with mental health conditions, the quote by Albert Einstein represents how the educational system has operated until now. The quote by Steve Jobs is where we're headed from today onward.

Each hour, day, month, and year offers new challenges and opportunities for leaders to make schools better. However, *better* is a relative term that requires careful planning, intense collaboration, accurate data analysis, credible stakeholder engagement, sufficient trial and error, ongoing training, and authentic reflection. Before bringing a new project, proposition, platform, procedure, or policy to life, educators must establish the pedagogical, psychological, and physical conditions for change. Having positive intentions isn't enough, especially when it comes to advancing equity for historically underserved students.

In the first iteration of the new initiative process in my book, *Leading the Launch*, I state that, "School leaders and district office administrators alike will benefit from learning ways to break through existing barriers, vet potential ideas, and create strategic plans for the effective execution of innovative tools, programs, or protocols in service to students" (Wallace, 2022, p. 3). This companion book will set forth a course of action to implement initiatives that help marginalized student groups by mitigating performance gaps and recapturing missed opportunities created and sustained by the system.

Figure I.1 details the ten consecutive steps for leaders as they launch any new initiative in their organizations. The process starts with researching and exploring various ideas with a team of collaborators who will help them examine the

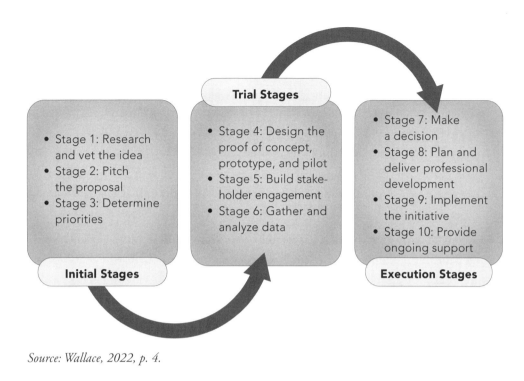

Source: Wallace, 2022, p. 4.

Figure I.1: Ten-stage process for new initiatives.

issues and see where the initiative might belong within the system. The project then moves into the trial stages to test its viability. When the initiative has been trialed for a predetermined period, adjustments will be made based on participant feedback and data analysis. After these first six stages, the leadership team will decide whether to implement the initiative. Once adopted by the organization, the last three stages provide the infrastructure to introduce the initiative into the school or district and institute procedures and mechanisms to support its long-term feasibility.

While most of the substance of and tools within this book are new, I may adapt or allude to references and resources from *Leading the Launch* (Wallace, 2022) at various points. While it's not critical to have read the previous book, it may help establish a deeper foundation for the content in this practitioner's guide. Either way, you choose.

IN THIS BOOK

If you are part of a school, district, county office, state department of education, or educational affiliate and have any role in implementing new initiatives, this book is for you. If you are someone who deeply cares about the well-being of young people and the future of our world, this book is for you. If you've experienced injustice, or have unknowingly benefited from it, and want to remedy preexisting systemic problems, this book is for you. This book is not about winners and losers. Victims or perpetrators. Personal blame or shame. There is no zero-sum game. I'm not the same teacher I was at age twenty-two or principal at thirty-five or superintendent at forty-eight, even—and I've made countless mistakes along the way (some inconsequential and some that still weigh heavily). But each year I commit myself to learning, questioning, listening, and evolving. And I strongly believe that's what we owe the students and families we have chosen to serve. This book is about knowing better, so we can do better.

Now that this introduction has established a clearer understanding of the historical context (including our own micro-history within it) on the road to educational and social justice, chapter 1 will help you develop insights into some modern-day barriers to equity embedded in the K–12 education system. You will be invited to lead your team through critical exercises to unearth potential stumbling blocks in your own setting. Then you'll be ready to strategize.

In the next six chapters, I condense and cluster each of the ten stages from *Leading the Launch* (Wallace, 2022) into new configurations, as the following describes (see also figure I.1, page 7).

- **Chapter 2, Initial Stages:** You'll start by investigating an equity-centered problem of practice and pitching a solution or approach that will address the inequity via a new initiative. After that, your team will collaborate and come to a consensus on how it might fit in the scheme of other district plans and priorities.

- **Chapter 3, Trial Stages:** Once past the preliminary stages, we will expand the equity-centered initiative by testing it out in a pilot experiment in a controlled setting. Then you'll reach out to early implementers and their subjects in the practice-run to gather data and feedback on the trial. From there, you will embark upon analyzing, making sense of, and reporting your findings.

- **Chapter 4, Decision-Making Stage:** Once you earn a green light for go, it's time to lay the groundwork to seek approval from your governing body, purchase training materials, and design the implementation rollout.

- **Chapter 5, Execution Stages:** After developing a high-quality, differentiated professional learning plan, you'll offer job-embedded technical training and pedagogical learning sessions for staff who will be implementing the initiative. Throughout the first year, a series of check-ins and adjustments are required, and you'll continue to monitor impact and keep people's focus on the initiative in the coming years.

- **Chapter 6, Making Space:** In this bonus step to the ten-stage process, leadership teams seek to identify equity-obstructive initiatives already in place that should be eliminated or altered to better attend to students' needs. This step also helps leaders balance resource management, reduce waste, and improve coherence throughout their institutions.

Each chapter includes a contemporary research base, hypothetical scenarios that demonstrate how equity-related goals and outcomes may show up in different educational settings, and reproducible handouts you can adapt or adopt as your team moves through the stages of the process. All right. Let's get to it.

CHAPTER 1

Barriers to Equity

The reality remains in 2023 that schools are still not meant for everyone—*yet*. That's why our work persists. My mission is to help leaders see that educational equity is not only possible but also probable, and someday even inevitable, when we focus in the right directions. It's well worth noting that personal predilections and obstacles are inevitable, but not always negative. We are not all meant to be microbiologists, chefs, filmmakers, mechanics, or lawyers. Thankfully, for society, myriad gifts and talents are incubating in each of us that can enrich the rest of us. So, the following section is not about making sure that everyone takes Mandarin, quantum physics, or Advanced Placement art history; only that the latent and budding symphony conductors, veterinarians, or ethnic studies professors have an institutionally supported pathway to strive for their particular niche in the world. And that we, as educators, are not standing in their way.

Before delving into the strategies and frameworks to execute equity-centered initiatives, it's critical to be aware of the barriers that both intentionally and unintentionally thwart progress toward organizational change. Three primary domains cast a wide net over the impediments educational leaders face in pursuing equitable outcomes for historically marginalized students (Wallace, 2012).

1. *First-order barriers* are easy to recognize because they are often functional or material in nature—it's the stuff we either don't have at all or don't have enough of, such as knowledge, skills, goods, or training.

2. *Second-order barriers* can be a bit sneaky because they take place in our brains, hearts, and spirits. They often emerge in words, behaviors, or expressions that suggest one's own attitudes or convictions are right and those who want them to change or think differently are wrong.

3. *Third-order barriers* are mostly human-made but not necessarily authored by the humans who still uphold them—they are spoken of almost as if they're inherently immovable but living entities, such as *the district, the master schedule, the standards,* or *the contract.*

In this chapter, we'll review the impact of the three tiers of barriers to equity and engage with questions for consideration about each. We will also reflect on past initiatives at your institution to begin devising a plan to avoid these barriers. The following scenarios help demonstrate how the three types of barriers manifest in real-life situations.

FIRST-ORDER BARRIERS: PHYSICAL OR OPERATIONAL

First-order barriers reflect physical or operational deficits that may include inadequate resources, time, equipment, services, or support to improve learning environments for students or working conditions for staff, especially in higher-needs communities. Meira Levinson, Tatiana Geron, and Harry Brighouse (2022) explain:

> Equity evaluators taking a resource-focused approach might ask whether girls attend as many days of school each year as boys; if low-income children have the same student-teacher ratios and curricular offerings as high-income children in the region; or whether textbooks, computers, or school nurses are available to refugee children at the same rate as they are available to children of citizens. One of the enduring and shameful features of schooling in the United States, for instance, is that schools and districts that disproportionately serve children who are low-income, non-White, noncitizen, and/or English language learners consistently have fewer resources and offer more limited curricular opportunities than do schools and districts that serve White, native-English-speaking children with US citizenship from middle- and upper-income families (Mathewson, 2020). In other words, the United States provides less to those who have less. We see similar patterns of difference if we compare spending across countries (UNESCO Institute for Statistics, 2022). (p. 3)

These systemic inequities are further exacerbated in that families with disposable income can supplement the basics that schools have to offer with private tutors, test prep, and higher quality medical and dental care, and regularly leverage other resources that further benefit their own children. This is why even though physical or operational barriers may seem low level or things that can be readily repaired by throwing money at them, they are incredibly crucial for those without significant means.

In addition, physical and operational barriers are often compounded and need to be addressed holistically, as exhibited in the following two hypothetical scenarios. After reviewing the scenarios about first-order barriers, discuss the corresponding questions in the reproducible at the end of the chapter (page 25) with your collaborative team.

Scenario One

> *Consider an elementary school that has launched a new after-school program that provides tutoring and homework help for academically struggling students. However, the buses from the transportation department—which primarily serve low-income families eligible for free or reduced-price meals—only pick up once an afternoon, just a few minutes after the last bell. The principal realizes the need to collaborate with the district office to see if the bus schedules can be adjusted to provide equitable access to the program, along with safe transportation home. Alternative partnerships are also investigated, such as coordinating neighborhood carpools and allocating funds to buy student passes for the public transportation system in lieu of district busing.*

Scenario Two

> *Each student in a middle school has been issued a laptop for home use, but many of the students have spotty or absent internet connectivity and cannot complete online homework assignments. The principal reaches out to the technology department to find out if hotspots can be purchased or if the district can work out a deal with local internet providers to supply free Wi-Fi in neighborhoods with the greatest concentration of socioeconomically disadvantaged families. In the meantime, teachers meet in their collaborative teams to design lessons that can be completed using the applications already downloaded onto student computers or provide assignment choices for students that don't rely solely on the internet.*

SECOND-ORDER BARRIERS: PEDAGOGICAL OR PSYCHOLOGICAL

This set of barriers refers to insufficient or obsolete knowledge, skills, beliefs, mindsets, and attitudes about teaching, learning, students, families (including, how schools should look or function), and the perceived benefits of preexisting models. For example, staff composition has a major influence on how students experience daily life at school. If the concept of "how we teach is how we (best) learned" rings true, then think about the people who go into education as a profession. It is not overwhelmingly composed of folks outside the mainstream: those who struggled to sit still in school, who were repeatedly punished for menial or major infractions, or who saw D's or F's land on their report cards. Educators are typically like you and me—the hall monitors, the spelling bee finalists, the library groupies, or the team players.

Furthermore, according to USA Facts (2020), most teachers come from dominant cultures or privileged backgrounds: highly educated (57 percent with a master's degree or higher); White (79 percent); and female (76 percent). Which leaves people of color, males of all races, socioeconomically disadvantaged people, and linguistically and ethnically diverse people on the outskirts. As a White teacher herself, Theresa Nomensen (2018) asserts, "White people assume they don't have a culture, everyone else does. White people are assumed to be normal and typical while people of color are ethnic, exotic, and different" (p. 23). This is not to say that White college-educated women are the problem, per se, as many were relegated to teaching as one of the very few professions open to them in the past. But they are the prototype for values, expectations, and customs we still often witness in modern classrooms.

While not a homogeneous demographic entirely, there are some hallmarks that permeate European descendants' middle class values that we see translated into traditional standards at school: cleanliness, self-discipline, orderliness, timeliness, and good manners—which entail sitting still in nice, neat rows of desks, standing quietly in line, and raising your hand to speak. None of these are bad practices by themselves, but should be expanded to encompass a greater range of values and, thereby, acceptance of wider expressions of learning and behaviors in our schools. Noisy classrooms bustling with engaged learners; social-emotional lessons on developing self-awareness and identity; dynamic, open-ended inquiry projects; restorative discipline practices; and other culturally responsive approaches are already broadening existing paradigms.

To loosely borrow the term from biosemiotics philosopher Jakob von Uexküll (1864–1944), *umwelt* refers to the theory that organisms that share the same environment possess wildly different worldviews and perspectives based on their sensory perceptions. "Every subject spins out, like the spider's threads, its relations to certain qualities of things and weaves them into a solid web, which carries its existence" (von Uexküll, 2010, p. 53). Another way of saying this is illustrated in the aphorism that "fish can't see the water they are swimming in" or "if you want to know what water is, don't ask a fish." Tim Elmo Feiten (2022) posits, "The concept of *Umwelt* thus performs a double duty . . . on the one hand the strictly empirical study of animal behavior and physiology, on the other hand a speculative and creative way of envisioning worlds radically different from ours" (p. 2). Employing the latter definition, humans exist in different *umwelten* depending on extreme variations between their existences on Earth. A feng shui consultant in China possesses distinct schema and environmental context from a performance artist in Canada, a video game tester in India, or a cattle rancher in Brazil. They each see, feel, taste, hear, and smell the world in ways that others may not, though we all inhabit the same biosphere.

In an adjacent example, Nereida Bueno-Guerra (2018) recalls:

> a popular vignette depicting some animals (a bird, a monkey, a penguin, an elephant, a fish, a seal and a dog) in front of a human interviewer in the middle of a savanna. The human says: "For a fair selection everybody has to take the same exam: please climb that tree." The core of the joke lies in the fact that the monkey is the unique animal among that group that could climb the tree and pass the exam. (p. 2)

This should not be considered a literal interpretation that students from diverse backgrounds are distinct species from each other or from their dominant-culture teachers; this only suggests that there is vast heterogeneity among us in how we learn and function that should be acknowledged, valued, and addressed rather than judged or unfairly assessed.

The following two scenarios illustrate how second-order barriers might show up in educational settings. After reviewing the scenarios about second-order barriers, discuss the corresponding questions in the reproducible at the end of the chapter (page 26) with your collaborative team.

Scenario One

> *The science curriculum council from a large suburban high school has been convening for a year to develop course pathways to meet the new locally determined graduation requirements. Every*

student must take three years of science in alignment with the national standards. The council recommends to the school board a three-tiered system for students to matriculate through the pathways beginning next fall. The only entry point is during the ninth-grade year, determined by a standardized test plus teacher recommendation. The curriculum council opposes open enrollment and multiple entry points, arguing that unprepared students would slow down the rest of the class, and they didn't want to set them up for failure—thus resulting in a tracked system that then affects all other course scheduling. The students in the least rigorous pathway also end up together in many of the other lowest-level English, social studies, and mathematics classes. The district's assessment department analyzes the placement data and reports that students of color and English learners are overrepresented in the most remedial pathway. The curriculum council's opinions must be challenged by an equity-centered school board whose votes on the pathway options will, ultimately, impact students' motivation to stretch themselves with more challenging material, meet four-year college admissions criteria, or pursue science-related fields in the future.

Scenario Two

A school district is attempting to adopt a new research-informed equity-centered grading policy based on Joe Feldman's book Grading for Equity *(2018), clearly outlining new expectations for both teachers and students. Staff in some academic departments are resisting the shift to restorative grading practices, which include a no-zeros component, elimination of letter grades on homework, and allowing students to retake tests until they demonstrate understanding. Administrators are fielding concerns from teachers that this new policy will infringe on their academic freedom and limit their ability to adequately cover the curriculum. They believe that students should be held responsible in some way, if not penalized, for not completing their homework: "Why would they do it otherwise?" These mindsets are indicative of holding on to past practices, regardless of what current research says about student learning and mastery of concepts. Therefore, the district must focus on sharing*

*compelling data and the rationale behind the changes to interrupt
outdated approaches and attitudes that suppress equity efforts
throughout the system.*

THIRD-ORDER BARRIERS: INSTITUTIONAL

These obstacles are situational, organizational, political, and structural, intent on protecting the status quo and stalling change efforts. They can be embedded in traditions, routines, schedules, procedures, and rules, or "just the way we do things around here." Again, it's risky to characterize this barrier within a good or bad binary: many of a school or district's ways of being build camaraderie, foster group identity, and honor their history. But while certain structures are necessary to organize complex systems so they function efficiently, safely, and cohesively, there are hidden dangers of valuing or elevating the institution over the individual.

School rules and policies tend to be rife with unconscious biases. Behavioral codes of conduct are frequently rooted in the intention to keep school campuses safe, orderly, and regulated. However, they can disproportionately impact segments of the population for reasons beyond their locus of control, such as the following.

- Dress codes can inadvertently discriminate against students who are in foster homes or experiencing homelessness, and who may not have the financial means to wear approved, clean, or school-defined appropriate clothing on a daily basis.

- Hair and grooming policies have been routinely weaponized against racial minorities and ethnic groups who don't conform with typically White conventions.

- Zero-tolerance discipline protocols often impact students who live in communities with gang violence and for whom carrying protection is not just the norm but essential for survival.

- Chronically truant students who are (paradoxically) punished with additional days of out-of-school suspension only fall further behind and become more disenfranchised from their teachers and peers.

The examples go on and on. That is why leaders must audit attendance and discipline data by demographics, closely examine their own assumptions, and respond to perceived student misdeeds on a case-by-case basis to actively dismantle bureaucratic structures that limit students' access to an equitable education.

After reviewing the following scenarios about third-order barriers, discuss the corresponding questions in the reproducible at the end of the chapter (page 27) with your collaborative team.

Scenario One

Prom season excitement is upon students at the local high school. Limos are reserved, dresses purchased and tuxes rented, and decorations for a magical evening assembled. Tickets go on sale six weeks before the main event: $35 for singles and $60 for couples. To incentivize good behavior in the senior class as they near graduation, the principal sends out a message that students who receive disciplinary consequences or have any unexcused absences will not be able to buy tickets. Furthermore, only opposite sex pairs may purchase tickets together as a couple; if same sex students want to attend together, they will need to buy single tickets and not "appear to be in a romantic relationship." Dance codes of conduct will be enforced as well, including requirements that males and females dress in "gender-conforming apparel." Chaperones will also reserve the right to remove students from the prom if they display "inappropriate behaviors on the dance floor," determined at the discretion of any supervising adult.

In response to the message, many students, with the support of their parents, decide to boycott the prom and hold an alternative public event in protest against: (1) the ticket price discrimination against LGBTQ+ couples and those without an opposite sex prom date, (2) using the prom as a behavior control mechanism, and (3) disallowing individual gender expression. What was meant to be a fun teenage rite of passage has turned into a draconian event that the seniors want no part of. The school leaders must decide whether to meet with the students and come to a compromise or risk public outrage at their rigid dictums.

Scenario Two

Even today, we hear of schools and districts that are battling to retain ethnically insensitive or racially bigoted mascots, caricatures, or imagery that many in their communities have traditionally held dear. In a rural middle school, a group of Indigenous students decides to petition the school board to change the school's mascot from the tomahawk-wielding character "Big Red" to a non-offensive name and object. At the board meeting, hundreds of longtime community members plea to keep the mascot intact. Many responses are emotionally charged and deep-seated. Some of their statements range from dismissive disregard ("It's just a harmless cartoon!"), to passive resistance ("It's not the right time; we have bigger fish to fry"), to outright defiance ("Over my dead body, will you take Big Red down!"). The school board has to decide whether to uphold the value of a fictitious symbol over the well-being of students. If they do, the inequity becomes sanctioned and codified and sends a message that tradition is to be upheld at whatever the cost to students and families. Alternatively, the board has an opportunity to replace the oppressive symbol and motto, perhaps with a local community hero who represents the diversity of the area and uplifts the district as an equity advocate.

REFLECT ON PAST INITIATIVES

As you can imagine, there is no shortage of scenarios that illustrate how the three levels of barriers can surface in educational environments. Hopefully, these fictional stories have helped you connect to situations in your own locales. Maybe your school or district has already faced private or public controversies related to inadequacy of resources (first-order), antiquated approaches (second-order), and outmoded models (third-order). Perhaps the current leadership has already hashed out the major misfires from the past or maybe you still need time to process what happened and why before moving forward.

The rest of this chapter contains two pre-stage process activities to orient leaders to how initiatives have been launched in the past and the conditions that may have contributed to missteps or failures in the implementation phase. The first activity invites you to revisit a restrictive or unjust initiative that may have been launched at your institution, review it, and observe what elements could have been redesigned for equity. The second activity prompts leadership teams to delve into their organizations to find the invisible ecosystems shaping district and school cultures and to better harness those elements in their equity-centered work.

INITIATIVE AUTOPSY

Your team will dissect a former initiative to examine how a certain program, policy, project, or process limited student access to an equitable education and what potential remedies could have interrupted the injustice (figure 1.1). (See page 28 for a blank reproducible version of this figure.) Revisiting situations that you've personally lived, learning from ones that preceded your tenure, or recalling cautionary tales from other places can all serve as a form of reflection that helps your team practice new mindsets with an equity lens.

ORGANIZATIONAL CULTURE ICEBERG

Many leaders are familiar with the concept of the "tip of the iceberg." It suggests that we can only see a small part of an enormous physical structure, while much more lies beneath the water. This metaphor is often used to illustrate conscious and unconscious ways of being in an organization. What you see above the waterline is the image or illusion that signifies the values and beliefs of a system. However, the way the system truly exists is submerged, saturated, and surrounded by intangible operating instructions. It is often those elusive rules or customs that undermine paths toward equity. Figures 1.2 (page 23) and 1.3 (page 24) illustrate this concept. (See page 29 for a blank reproducible version of figure 1.3)

---

1. Briefly describe an initiative (for example, a program, policy, curriculum, or procedure) that your school, district, or organization attempted to implement that (intentionally or unintentionally) created barriers to educational equity.

To try to improve the district's graduation rates and state standings in the comparative schools' rankings during No Child Left Behind, the school board adopted a policy in which every student who turns eighteen during the spring semester and is not on track to graduate by that June would be involuntarily transferred to the district's continuation high school or placed in the independent study program, both of which require fewer credits to meet graduation requirements. At the time, the school board believed it would be positive for both the district's graduation rates and for credit-deficient students who would be able to earn a diploma within four years. The counselors met with each family and presented only two options, categorically denying students a third option to stay enrolled at their home school site. However, neither of the alternative education settings were accredited and earning a diploma from those campuses would prevent students from applying to a four-year college, thus limiting their postsecondary options to community college or trade school.

2. What contributed to the initiative's downfall?

While the program wasn't originally on the radar of most of the district's staff and teachers, administrators and counselors at the traditional and alternative high schools began to meet quarterly to assess how the program was going. Within the first year, many red flags arose about the attrition and dropout rates from the involuntarily transferred students. School leaders began to collect data and analyze the demographics more closely. Of the eighteen-year-olds identified for the programs, 58 percent were low-income males and 73 percent from limited-English speaking backgrounds. The continuation high school and independent study programs had no bilingual teachers or English-language development specialists on site so even if the students did show up to campus, they did not receive adequate support services to meet their learning goals.

3. What were the resulting impacts on students, staff, or both?

When forced to leave their familiar environments and given little to no choice about their fate (compounded by the fact that eighteen-year-olds are considered adults and no longer required to attend school) over 65 percent of the students neglected to show up at their new school assignment and dropped out. The students were essentially pushed out of school prematurely, which was the exact opposite of the intention behind the program. Many of the home school teachers of the transferred students protested the policy because they understood that removing students from the campus where they had strong peer and staff relationships would be contrary to the goal of the policy. They advocated for allowing the students to stay on an extra semester to gain the skills they needed to go out into the world. The high school principals reported their findings to the superintendent, who drafted an agenda item for the next school board meeting.

Figure 1.1: Initiative autopsy.

continued ▶

4. How, if at all, were the harmful effects mitigated?

The school board, appalled by the outcomes, suspended the program immediately for the second year and established a task force comprised of students, parents, and school staff to study the many underlying issues. They also directed staff to personally invite students who had been detrimentally affected to attend an additional semester at their comprehensive high school to finish their credits and graduate. While most students did not accept this offer because they'd moved on with their lives, 12 percent did return and earned an accredited diploma. Furthermore, by emphasizing how many English learners were disproportionately enrolled in alternative education programs, the school board authorized senior management to allocate appropriate staffing to each school for language acquisition support.

5. In hindsight, what might have been done differently during the implementation process to yield greater positive impacts on student groups?

Before making any policy decisions fueled by ranking or competition with other districts, the school board might have examined the problem more closely before creating a solution that only theoretically seemed to work. They could have asked the director of secondary education to present several options with pros and cons they could select from so the decision would take into consideration many more factors and impacts on students. If they had started with an eye on equity, further damage to already marginalized students could have been prevented.

Chipping Away at the Iceberg

Directions: Referring to the following image, Identify the potential obstacles that your equity-centered initiative is likely to encounter in your own environment.

The Iceberg That Sinks Organizational Change

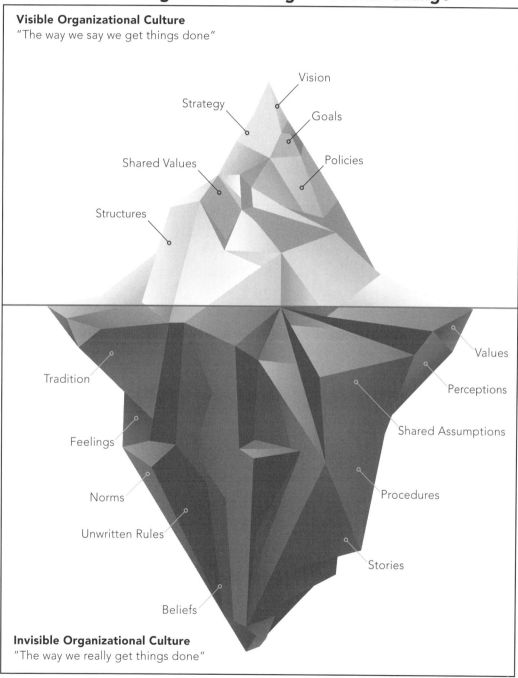

Source: © 2014 by Torben Rick. Used with permission.

Figure 1.2: Organizational culture is like an iceberg.

Tip of the Iceberg "The way we say we get things done."	Beneath the Surface "The way we really get things done."
School or district mission and vision statements	What people really believe
Official leadership structure or organization chart	De facto power structure
Key school board or district goals	Private or interest group agendas
Sanctioned process to adopt new programs	Actual ways new programs get chosen
Messages we send to students and families	Hidden meanings or implied messages
How we say we serve *all* students	How we really serve *some* students differently
Who we say we are	Who we really act like we are
Who we want to be	
How our team will address the invisible organizational culture by leveraging the visible culture to advance equity	

Figure 1.3: Unpacking the organizational iceberg.

CONCLUSION

Though what you've discovered about your school or district in this chapter may initially feel discouraging or even demoralizing, it's actually quite promising. The skeletons are finally out of the closet. Once what's hidden is exposed, you can start to confront the challenges ahead consciously and intentionally. Chapter 2 (page 31) will get you started on the process of identifying the student groups most harmed by your organization's existing practices, policies, and programs and devising some initial ideas for how to dismantle those damaging structures. After you've narrowed in on a particular problem you want to tackle, you can begin to visualize solutions for a better way forward.

First-Order Barriers: Questions for Consideration

In the hypothetical scenarios regarding first-order barriers on page 13, what are some additional barriers that might not be immediately visible that could impact student access to higher quality learning experiences?

What are some of the compounding operational barriers prevalent in your own school or district that sometimes get in the way of increasing equity for students and families?

Think about a time when you were told that something was not possible due to physical constraints. What was it and what options might have been reconsidered to help you proceed with your equity-related goal?

What untapped or underutilized resources in your community might be available to help you overcome first-order barriers?

Second-Order Barriers: Questions for Consideration

What kinds of implicit messages are being communicated to students and families in the hypothetical scenarios regarding second-order barriers on page 15?

What are some of the key refrains or euphemisms you hear in your school or district that represent deficit thinking, fixed mindsets, or protection of existing conditions such as "it's always worked before, why change now?" or "we should stick to what we know"?

What are the biggest equity-related second-order truths people are unwilling to acknowledge in your setting that impede progress or change?

To what extent has your organization changed because of the COVID-19 pandemic in terms of how people believe schools should exist and function? How have the shifts resulted in increased or decreased equitable conditions for students?

Third-Order Barriers:
Questions for Consideration

What current events or news stories have you heard recently that relate to school policies, safety measures, or ritual and legacy and resemble the hypothetical scenarios on page 18?

In your own community, have you heard people say: "It's the [school, district, or city] way?" Who usually says it? When does it typically come up? What does it explicitly or implicitly suggest?

What kinds of structures are in place in your own environment that present institutional barriers to advancing equity?

While the COVID-19 pandemic that began in 2020 interrupted many preexisting practices and routines and required third-order change, were modifications made that prioritized equity? Were there any unintended consequences that created additional barriers for marginalized students?

Initiative Autopsy

1. Briefly describe an initiative (for example, a program, policy, curriculum, or procedure) that your school, district, or organization attempted to implement that (intentionally or unintentionally) created barriers to educational equity.

2. What contributed to the initiative's downfall?

3. What were the resulting impacts on students, staff, or both?

4. How, if at all, were the harmful effects mitigated?

5. In hindsight, what might have been done differently during the implementation process to yield greater positive impacts on student groups?

Unpacking the Organizational Culture Iceberg

Tip of the Iceberg "The way we say we get things done."	Beneath the Surface "The way we really get things done."
School or district mission and vision statements:	What people really believe:
Official leadership structure or organization chart:	De facto power structure:
Key school board or district goals:	Private or interest group agendas:
Sanctioned process to adopt new programs:	Actual ways new programs get chosen:
Messages we send to students and families:	Hidden meanings or implied messages:

page 1 of 2

Tip of the Iceberg "The way we say we get things done."	Beneath the Surface "The way we really get things done."
How we say we serve *all* students:	How we really serve *some* students differently:
Who we say we are:	Who we really act like we are:
Who we want to be:	
How our team will address the invisible organizational culture by leveraging the visible culture to advance equity:	

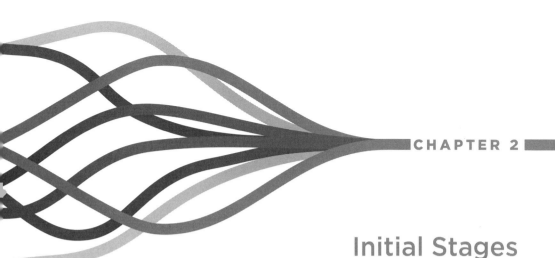

Initial Stages

The first three stages of the ten-stage process for advancing equity in a district initiative include pinpointing and situating the problem of practice that the new initiative intends to solve. You have likely been pondering ways to improve academic, social-emotional, or developmental outcomes for one or more minoritized groups of students at your school or district. As the initiator of the proposition, you will start with stage 1 by engaging in a self-study on the topic through reading, listening, observing, and pondering. Once a distinct idea begins to crystallize, you will invite others into the conversation during stage 2. The team you assemble will listen to your proposal, provide critical feedback, and then send you back to the drawing board. If momentum continues to flow, the team will then review all other initiatives already in progress and those waiting in the wings in the stage 3 prioritization process. These steps combined serve as the foundation for moving the plan into the trial period outlined in chapter 3 (page 61). In this chapter, we review investigative options for determining the nature of your initiative by studying existing problems, preparing a pitch, tuning your protocols, analyzing the results of previous initiatives for opportunities to revisit, and prioritizing multiple initiatives for a more organized implementation.

> ## KEY CONCEPTS
>
> **Stage 1: Investigate.** Pinpoint the problem of practice your initiative will solve.
>
> **Stage 2: Pitch.** Create a formal proposal for consideration.
>
> **Stage 3: Prioritize.** Decide order of implementation for your district initiative.

STAGE 1: INVESTIGATE

The first stage is to interrogate the past, investigate the present, and imagine the future for your most vulnerable populations. Formal research, including a literature review related to the topic of study, may help leaders formulate questions to ask and future directions to consider. Circumstantial research, such as exploring similar programs or projects other districts or local communities have undertaken, also benefits this stage of the process. You should approach the investigation stage without being too attached to any outcomes. In other words, take in the information you find out without judgment or early conclusions. It's important to remain curious and open-minded and not try to parse out the pros and cons quite yet. Be open to new information that might conflict with what you thought you knew. You will engage in that discernment process later. For now, you are here to learn.

According to the Carnegie Project on the Education Doctorate's (CPED; n.d.) framework, a *problem of practice* is "a persistent, contextualized, and specific issue embedded in the work of a professional practitioner, the addressing of which has the potential to result in improved understanding, experience, and outcomes." To be clear, inequities must be framed as problems of practice, *not* as problems with any particular student group related to racial, ethnic, or linguistic background, familial composition, or exhibited behaviors. At this point in the process, the true causes of a problem may not yet be well understood and, if we aren't careful, can lead to exacerbation of the problem or misguided attempts to confront an incorrectly defined issue. A perfect example of this is shown in figure 1.1 (p. 20) in the initiative autopsy example. The school board sincerely believed they were offering a remedy to the district's graduation rates dilemma, but the results were highly detrimental to an already distressed group of students on the verge of not graduating, and consequently harmed their future options. Unlike the miscalculating school board though, you are going to put many more protections into place before impacting actual students. Don't worry if you don't get it immediately right. This is only your first attempt of many at defining the problem of practice you will address in your initiative to advance equity.

Figure 2.1 is an example tool to help you start to investigate a problem of practice that will later be brought to your team. (See page 53 for a blank reproducible version of this figure.)

STUDYING THE PROBLEM

Most educators are eager and natural students; for this first step into the initial stages, it's time to flex your college research muscles. Luckily, your master's

Equity-Centered Problem of Practice	Resources to Understand the Problem of Practice	Potential Initiatives to Address the Problem of Practice
School nutrition services has alerted the superintendent and the school board that food insecurity among immigrant students has tripled in the past year.	• Collect information from the school nutrition services database and student information system to determine scope of need. • Develop a list of contacts for community-based organizations that have food pantries or no-cost meals. • Identify other compounding issues facing immigrant families.	• In addition to the federally funded free breakfast and lunch, find ways to involve community organizations to supply dinner, weekend, or both family meals. • Involve students in creating a community garden, kitchen, or canteen to supply healthy, free foods near immigrant centers.
The current literacy pull-out model for English learners in the elementary schools causes students to miss other core academic instruction and social activities.	• Evaluate the existing models at each school to calibrate how interventions are delivered and what their scheduling conflicts might be. • Read the latest research on English language development strategies. • Ask the county office or state department of education for recommendations.	• Implement an English language development literacy program that can be done alongside native English speakers during the language arts block. • Purchase online licenses for English learners to participate in literacy practice outside school. • Redesign all elementary master schedules to ensure equitable access to social activities.
The Healthy Kids Survey indicates low-income seventh-grade girls are experiencing disproportionately higher levels of mental health concerns compared to all other groups.	• Investigate the data to learn more about what kinds of mental health issues are most prominent. • Review literature on adolescent female development. • Contact school counselors to ascertain whether what they are seeing corroborates the findings.	• Add a new course or section on healthy coping skills to the middle school curriculum. • Create an after-school support network for female students. • Update services plan to better assist low-income families with mental health options.

Figure 2.1: Equity-centered problems of practice.

thesis or dissertation are behind you—and if not, maybe this could be your area of study! Regardless, conducting action research that can potentially improve students' lives makes your undertaking that much more compelling and rewarding. The following supporting material from stage 1 of *Leading the Launch* (Wallace, 2022) has been updated to include the equity stance and is the next step in getting to the roots of your problem of practice. In preparation for pitching the proposal in stage 2, the leader should be able to provide high-level answers to the following six prompts.

1. Identify the current or emerging rationale for developing the initiative to increase equitable outcomes for students.

2. Develop awareness and alignment with other equity-focused district strategic plans.

3. Tap into the history and background that have produced or sustained past inequities.

4. Forecast the future related to how this initiative will advance learning conditions for historically underserved students.

5. Anticipate the impact on and reaction of stakeholders, including those toward whom the initiative is geared, and those toward whom it is not.

6. Brainstorm estimated costs and identify current or untapped funds or resources that can be reallocated toward increasing equity.

Let's consider that your district has been identified by the county office of education as overidentifying and placing Black male students in special education settings. In reviewing the data, you find out that over 50 percent of these placements indicate behavioral challenges or perceived disorders, while all other subgroups are well under 10 percent. This basic information is an overt red flag of an equity dilemma that needs immediate attention. Addressing the six prompts will help you develop strategies to meet Black male students' learning goals in order to reduce behaviors that are triggering over-representation in special education. Table 2.1 illustrates how the first stage of the process might unfold.

As you can see from the hypothetical scenario in table 2.1, stage 1 consists of knowledge and resources that serve to help you formulate which initial ideas to pursue. There are many missing pieces of information that still need to be gathered to formulate the pitch in stage 2. You may have several potential initiatives cropping up that you need to choose from or combine into one. The next activity will help you prime your pitch for presentation.

Table 2.1: Studying the Problem

Prompt	Current Status	Ideas to Explore
1. Identify the current or emerging rationale for developing the initiative to increase equitable outcomes for students.	The county office has directed the district to develop a plan to address the disproportionality of Black male students exhibiting behavior issues that result in special education placements.	• Find other similarly situated districts that have been successful in reducing identification and placements. • Ask the county for additional resources or leads they might have to support our intentions to rectify the problem. • Conduct research to educate ourselves more on the issue.
2. Develop awareness and alignment with other equity-focused district strategic plans.	Our district has three separate plans related to reducing inequities in our educational services to families: (1) the local control accountability plan, (2) the differentiated assistance plan, and (3) the 21st Century Scholar Blueprint.	• The local accountability plan has two goals directly related to advancing equity for underserved students. We can add specific actions related to Black male student success. • The differentiated assistance plan calls out our district's requirement to find alternatives to suspension and expulsion of students of color; perhaps we can extend this intention to reducing special education designations as well. • The 21st Century Scholar Blueprint was developed by our school board to prepare students for postgraduation success. We could align the behavioral and life skills portion to the initiative we might develop to advance equity for Black male students.
3. Tap into the history and background that have produced or sustained past inequities.	Our district originally had very few students of color and is now shifting demographically. Most of our teachers have been in the district for over a decade. They have not been introduced to culturally responsive methodologies or the latest research on managing classroom behaviors. In short, the student population has changed, but the staff has not been explicitly expected to teach or handle issues that arise with an equity lens.	• We need to share demographic changes in our community with school staff to help them recognize the need for new approaches. • Historically, students have been placed in courses based on teacher recommendation, including behavior and grades. Are there other ways we can broaden our view of students to open new academic pathways and also support teachers in expanding their thinking? • I've heard of district equity audits that can help discover exactly where the core problems are rooted. Let's find out more about what is out there and how it might be implemented.

continued ▲

Prompt	Current Status	Ideas to Explore
4. Forecast the future related to how this initiative will advance learning conditions for historically underserved students.	We are charged with reducing the number of Black male students on Individualized Education Plans (IEPs) and 504 Plans down to the average for all other subgroups (about 10 percent). This initiative will create new mechanisms for managing behaviors at the lowest levels in the classroom to reduce referrals for escalated interventions—which, in many cases, have ultimately resulted in moving students from mainstream classes into more restrictive environments.	• Many positive outcomes could emerge from this endeavor. Teachers will learn additional tools to create a supportive and safe learning environment for all students in their classrooms. • Students will learn life and coping skills that can translate to higher education and future work situations. • Special education services will be appropriately sized for the district and be able to focus resources on students who will truly benefit from specialized programming.
5. Anticipate the impact on and reaction of stakeholders, including those toward whom the initiative is geared, and those toward whom it is not.	This initiative is a result of a mandate from the county office of education. It may feel punitive or obligatory to some—just a box to check off. For others, there may be feelings of deprivation or inadequacy, possibly even frustration expressed as anger. However, there are also some fierce equity advocates who will be excellent ambassadors for taking a stance to do right by our students.	• This is a hard one. I'm sure there will be resistance to making widespread changes that will impact the whole system. We need to make sure our communication of the initiative is culturally sensitive and refrains from victim blaming. • It's important that we make sure that the rationale is clear and that people will be supported through the change. The leadership team must anticipate resistance that may arise and proactively have responses ready to educate the communities affected in compassionate and satisfying ways.
6. Brainstorm estimated costs and identify current or untapped funds or resources that can be reallocated toward increasing equity.	• The estimated costs for teacher training, behavior specialist support, and class size reduction (to decrease staff-to-student ratios to a reasonable level) will cost approximately $600,000. • As part of our differentiated assistance plan, we have been allocated $295,000 to execute any initiative that results in expected improvements toward our goals. • By appropriately placing students on IEPs, we will be able to recover at least $300,000 due to reducing special education paraeducators and teachers in classrooms across the district.	• We can investigate purchasing programs such as Positive Behavioral Interventions and Supports (PBIS), or others on the topic of culturally responsive practices, or we can create our own versions. Either way, we will need to allocate ongoing funding for professional development and capacity building. I will reach out to instructional services to find out if there are upcoming grants that can be used for these purposes. • The differentiated assistance funding will only last as long as we are *not* meeting our goals. We need to find out what the county can offer to keep our positive momentum going via other funding avenues.

PREPARING TO PITCH

Have you heard the saying "It's a whole new ball game?" This phrase implies that strategies used in the past may need to be changed for different circumstances, which is an apt metaphor for executing equity-centered initiatives. In the game of baseball, pitchers traditionally use the *windup* method to get into motion and establish a rhythm before throwing the ball. Pitchers achieve the windup position when they put their leading foot on the rubber and face the batter with both shoulders. They prepare to deliver the ball by winding it backward like a spring and using the front foot as support when they swing their arm overhead to unleash the ball. As they square off with the batter at home plate, they communicate with the catcher to determine which pitch to throw and then decide on the best strategy to get the opposing player out.

This analogy can also be applied to preparing for pitching your proposal in stage 2. To narrow down the investigation, the leader (as pitcher) needs to answer the key questions in figure 2.2 (page 38) ahead of game day. (See page 54 for a blank reproducible of this figure.) Practice makes perfect, so spend some time anticipating what the rest of the team will need from you as you warm up. You may want to select one close colleague to toss your ball of ideas back and forth with prior to the main event.

As you can see, stage 1 is all about questions and answers. It's a process of:

- Interrogating your problem of practice, then more asking more questions

- Researching the topic, then forming clearer avenues

- Crystallizing some approaches, then forming more sophisticated inquiries

- Landing on a potential initiative, then winding up for the pitch

STAGE 2: PITCH

The first stage is the only stage that is a solo mission; the remainder require collaboration. District leaders must do their homework before they can develop anything concrete. Even new initiatives don't exist within a vacuum, but are surrounded by environmental context and institutional memory. One of the main casualties that new leaders or leaders in new roles or locations face is not figuring out the lay of the land before acting. It's exceedingly easy to criticize a past decision only to find out the individual who developed it (and who may be above you on the power structure) hears of your criticism, or even worse, you've accidentally

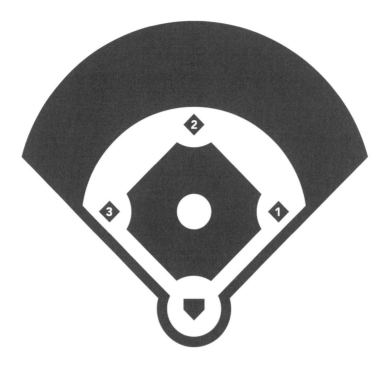

1. What is the specific initiative that I'm proposing? (A resource? A process? A program? A training? A system? A policy?)

2. What needs to be communicated, to whom, and how?

3. What are the stats (data) I need to share with the rest of the team?

4. What questions, comments, or opinions may come out of left field?

 5. Why do I believe this initiative will help level the playing field for identified student groups?

Figure 2.2: Winding up the pitch.

said it right to the person's face. Losing potential allies from the get-go is not a stellar approach, so spend some time learning about the evolution of the implementation you wish to change or enact. And when the time comes, be ready to show (objectively) how adaptations or revisions might help to focus the equity lens and respond to today's students in innovative and exciting ways.

It bears repeating from *Leading the Launch* that some new initiatives, such as the one depicted in figure 2.1 (page 33), are warranted by mandate rather than on a voluntary basis. In a perfect world, we would naturally pursue educational equity as part of our moral calling as educators. But that's not always the case and, for our purposes here, the implementation process is one and the same. No matter the source behind your initiative, there will always be advocates; there will always be detractors, and there will always be those watching from the sidelines. What matters most is finding solutions to our most pressing social inequities. And how you do this best is with a team.

THE NUANCES OF EQUITY-CENTERED COLLABORATIVE TEAMS

Collaboration is a ubiquitous buzzword in education. So is the custom of collaborative teamwork. Often school and district groupings are predetermined by role such as grade level, instructional leadership, subject area, and department team. This is your opportunity to rethink and reconstitute the teaming concept, one which is designated for a limited period for a specific purpose. This team is not inherited or preordained, but one that you get to inaugurate and facilitate as well as conclude. Since the focus is on equity, equitable membership should form the basis of your selection process.

Composition is paramount. People who are experienced, knowledgeable, and ethnically, linguistically, and culturally diverse, and invested in the cause should be at the table alongside those who may be tasked with implementation (if they are not the same people). Including people of differing ethnic and religious backgrounds, age groups, and abilities, as well as people along the spectrum of sexual orientation and gender identity will also help create an unbiased team. However, solicitations to join should not be gratuitous or smack of tokenism— don't just invite someone because they are, for example, nonbinary, a millennial, or Muslim. And please don't ask them to represent or speak for "their people" once on the team.

Do ask everyone to commit to participate fully to the best of their ability and exhibit respect and value for all contributions, whether their own ideas make it to final version or not. This can be accomplished by collectively developing team norms in the first meeting and honoring those throughout the process. There are many ways to craft norms and most leaders have done so many times before, but if you need some help, the Center for Creative Leadership (2020) is an outstanding resource to refer to (see www.ccl.org/articles/leading-effectively-articles /the-real-world-guide-to-team-norms).

A few final words about teams. Though this frank piece of advice comes from the business world, it also applies to the educational arena. Forbes contributor Mark Murphy (2015) breaks it down as follows:

> Forget about the Antagonists at first and put the initial focus on your Champions. Because if you start where you already have a strong base of support, your Champions will spread that message throughout their vast networks, building the strong platform you need. . . . There's also a hidden danger in attempting to tackle your weakest supporters first. Because if you make your pitch and it falls flat, and the Antagonists decide they're not going to support you, you've just effectively built up a well of angry people. And that puts your Champions in a tough spot. They may not be looking for a knock-down-drag-out battle with an equally powerful person who is 100% against you.

As you are barely out of the gate in stage 2, you certainly don't want your noble cause to fail this early on.

TUNING PROTOCOL

After distilling the collected resources and forming some tentative conclusions about their meaning in stage 1, the team leader then creates a formal proposal. They convene a meeting with the team members they've identified and guide them through a tuning protocol to uncover gaps and flaws in the first iteration. Tuning protocols have been used by groups of teachers to analyze student work and make improvements to their instructional lessons since the 1990s. "Initially developed by the Coalition of Essential Schools . . . the tuning protocol is a form of collective inquiry that allows participants to work together on improving student learning" (Easton, 2002). Administrators can modify the tool as needed to examine their own leadership practices in support of school or district protocols.

Since equity is the critical component, the tuning protocol should heavily focus on concrete, equity-related results. The primary objective is to obtain feedback about whether an equity-centered initiative has been prepared enough to move into the third stage. The protocol in figure 2.3, from *Leading the Launch* (Wallace, 2022) has been revised to home in on expected equity outcomes.

When you tune a plan, you have two basic components: a set of *equity-driven* goals, and activities sequenced in a way that helps your group meet *explicit* intentions. The objective is to get feedback from colleagues about the degree to which the activities seem likely to help the group foster increased equitable outcomes. The plan is in tune when the goals and activities are in alignment. This is also critical for your new initiative to move into the implementation stage.

Leader's Presentation (fifteen minutes):

- ☐ Description of equity-centered initiative

- ☐ Why you believe this initiative will better support underserved students

- ☐ How the initiative aligns with existing district frameworks, initiatives, and mission

- ☐ Data revealing gaps between student groups that warrant attention

- ☐ The intended impacts on improving curriculum, instruction, and student learning for identified student groups

- ☐ How you will measure those impacts on identified student groups

- ☐ The anticipated timeline from conception to full launch

- ☐ Resources and expertise needed (personnel, training, materials, technology, time) that exist within and outside the system

- ☐ Stakeholder engagement and ample outreach opportunities to connect with historically marginalized groups

- ☐ Regular and accessible communications (including translations, plain language) in multiple formats

Clarifying Questions (three minutes):

- ☐ Clarifying questions pertain to matters that can be answered factually or in a few short words. Save substantive issues for later.

- ☐ The protocol facilitator, not the presenter, is responsible for making sure that clarifying questions are actually clarifying.

Individual Feedback (two minutes):

- ☐ Participants write down *warm* and *cool* feedback to share in the whole-group discussion.

- ☐ They can phrase warm feedback as "I like . . ." or "I appreciate . . ." to show favorable reactions.

- ☐ They can phrase cool feedback as "I wonder . . ." or "You may consider . . ." to prompt further thinking and discussion.

Figure 2.3: Tuning protocol.

continued ▶

Group Feedback (fifteen minutes:)

☐ Participants talk to each other about the presenter's plan (as if the presenter is not in the room, to ensure that their commentary is about the ideas, not the individual), beginning with the ways the plan seems likely to meet the goals, continuing with possible disconnects and problems, and perhaps ending with one or two probing questions for further reflection by the presenter.

Presenter Reaction (five minutes):

☐ The presenter talks about what was learned from the team's feedback. This is not a time to defend oneself, but a time to explore further interesting ideas that came out of the feedback section. At any point, the presenter may open the conversation to the entire group (or not).

Next Steps and Debrief (five minutes):

☐ The team discusses next steps for the initiative.

☐ The facilitator leads an open discussion of this tuning experience.

---

*Visit **go.SolutionTree.com/diversityandequity** for a free reproducible version of this figure.*

POSTGAME ANALYSIS

After conducting the tuning protocol, the team leader examines the feedback and considers the critiques offered. It may very well be that this earliest version of the plan is inadequate, needs significant development, or doesn't clearly address the identified equity concerns. Team leaders then must decide whether to continue to cut their losses in pursuit of other projects. However, if there is sufficient enthusiasm, interest, or momentum, team leaders should seek answers to outstanding questions and revise their draft proposal into a blueprint for action.

To take the baseball metaphor just one step further, reporters often do postgame interviews with players immediately after a contest. Major scoring plays and errors are discussed as well as overall reflections on the game and what to work on in the future. The following activity is designed for team leaders to capture their own fresh reactions to help solidify the next stage in their game plan.

A *SWOT analysis* is a technique to assess your fledgling initiative using the four aspects that comprise the acronym: *strengths, weaknesses, opportunities,* and *threats.* Though originally designed for the marketplace, a literature review conducted by business professors and lecturers Mostafa Ali Benzaghta, Abdulaziz Elwalda, Mousa Mohamed Mousa, Ismail Erkan, and Mushfiqur Rahman (2021) reveals that higher education began to incorporate "SWOT as a convenient tool at the evaluation stage in order to gain an initial idea of possible future consequences" (p. 58). The SWOT grid can easily be applied to the K–12 setting with some adaptations for our purposes. Most use this tool in the business world at later stages of strategic planning. Instead, we will be using it the early stages by extracting components from the tuning protocol (see figure 2.3, page 41), as shown in figure 2.4. (See page 55 for a blank reproducible version of this figure.)

Directions: Summarize your impressions from the tuning protocol discussion in the four boxes.

Strengths (warm feedback; positive comments; areas of enthusiasm)	Opportunities (clarity; connections; synchronicity)
Weaknesses (cool feedback; negative comments; areas of disinterest or apathy)	Threats (disconnects; confusion; apprehensions)
Reflections	
Do the strengths and opportunities to advance equity outweigh the weaknesses and threats? If not, can the balance be shifted with some adaptations?	
Do I now feel more, less, or the same commitment to seeing this initiative move forward?	
Does it have enough initial support from others to bring it to stage 3, prioritization?	
Recommendation	

Figure 2.4: Post pitch SWOT analysis.

If everything seems to align thus far in stages 1 and 2, then you can feel confident bringing the initiative to the prioritization stage. If not, do a bit more digging. Remember that there is no time limit to any stage in the process, but there should be a sense of urgency to do as much as possible to serve the students we have sitting in our classrooms.

STAGE 3: PRIORITIZE

Once the team agrees that the reworked initiative is ready to compete with preexisting implementations as well as other new ideas, it enters the prioritization stage. In this phase, the leadership team takes a critical look at all of the school, department, or district's current initiatives. By outlining the commitments that the organization has already made and charting the progress of those initiatives in relationship to each other, leaders will gain a different, wider outlook. In *Leading the Launch* (Wallace, 2022), I note the following:

> Increasing equity for diverse student populations must be a serious determinant in the appraisal of any new initiative. If we don't have a sharp eye on equity, we may select a program, product, or service that actually widens achievement gaps between different groups instead of closing them. It's not enough to do no harm; those developing new initiatives must intentionally seek out or develop initiatives that meet the specific needs of particular learners. (p. 44)

Furthermore, we can learn how to practically apply the concept of balancing preexisting initiatives alongside new ones. The funnel images in figure 2.5 and figure 2.6 (page 46) contain multiple implementations that one might find in a typical school district. The prioritization process helps organize the flow of each project or program so it doesn't bottleneck and get trapped in the narrow opening.

The original version of the funnel from *Leading the Launch* (figure 2.5) focused on serving *all* students regardless of past insufficiencies, harm, or unmet demands. The funnel in figure 2.6 (page 46) contains several equity-centered initiatives that:

- Call out specific groups that have been underrepresented in the past in specific areas (such as girls in STEM professions) or have been oppressed by legislation or de facto policies (such as native speakers of other languages being forced to speak English only or risk punishment)

- Offer customized programming or support that pertains to the group's particular needs (for example, providing age-appropriate

Source: Wallace, 2022, p. 38.

Figure 2.5: Managing multiple implementations.

    sexual health information to LBGTQ+ students or child rearing instruction for expecting parents)

- Honor, legitimize, and foster pride in certain groups' existences that may have been previously invisible or historically subjugated (such as most cultures outside the White, heterosexual majority)

- Normalize and spread principles of diversity that benefit everyone in the organization and increase inclusivity between groups that have been previously separated or segregated via master scheduling or ability tracking (such as special education from regular education classrooms or English learners from English speakers)

- Create opportunities for postsecondary success, self-sufficiency, and vitality including career readiness, financial literacy, and basic skills support for students with special needs or from low socioeconomic backgrounds

- Establish positive roles for teachers and staff of color or other minority status and expand knowledge and awareness of unfamiliar cultures for those in the majority

- Destigmatize difference and cultivate compassion

Figure 2.6: Managing multiple equity-centered implementations.

The beauty of equity-centered initiatives is that the possibilities are endless: you can mix and match groups with various permutations and integrate students and adults in novel configurations. We want to be careful, however, to avoid inadvertently recreating or perpetuating segregating conditions by strictly limiting who can be involved in distinct endeavors, while still holding the sanctity of spaces that create affinity and connection between marginalized students of the same identity. Remember, equity is not equality. When in doubt, consult with the targeted audience to gauge their feelings about an open versus closed approach.

Recalling Paul Gorski's (2019) equity detours from the introduction (page 1), equity-centered initiatives should not be or be perceived merely as add-ons, extracurriculars, or electives. That said, depending on the political climate of your district, these may be the earliest entry points to the eventual transformation of the adopted curriculum or mainstream program of study to include and represent voices that have traditionally been on the periphery. Law six of Peter Senge's (2006) Eleven Laws of Systems Thinking is *Faster is slower*, as in, "the optimal rate is far less than the fastest possible growth" (p. 62). This simply means that pacing is important, and that, while we can't necessarily wait for those with privilege to advance causes they initially see no benefit from, we must do our best to show them compelling evidence, data, or other motivators to accept that we are going to engage in change efforts, regardless of their degree of comfort with them.

One way of doing this is to consider how the new equity goal might complement or be embedded in already adopted implementations. Figure 2.7 (page 48) demonstrates how a team might vet the various initiatives with an eye on equity to predict the level of impact on the intended student groups.

Not every district initiative will affect the student groups you're focused on. The point is not to force-fit new ideas into old paradigms, but rather to expand your thinking to implementations already in process that can be authentically leveraged and bridged to the new initiative. For instance, in figure 2.7 (page 48), two areas are deemed high impact on the targeted group and several medium designations could be elevated to high. So, if the new initiative you are considering provides additional transportation options for families in rural areas to improve student attendance, the impact may be positively compounded by simultaneously updating the attendance policy to include leniency for late buses and trains and ensuring that the wellness center hours of operation will accommodate family work schedules. Removing the silo effect that typically happens in schools and districts makes the system function more efficiently and effectively.

PRIORITIZING INITIATIVES

Associate professor of psychiatry and behavioral sciences at the University of Washington Jill Locke and colleagues (2019) studied how evidence-based practices (EBP) for embedding mental health services in schools intersect with organizational implementation. Simply put, how does a new initiative to offer mental health services on campuses impact climate, leadership, citizenship, and behavior? Among their findings is that competing priorities between academic and social-emotional programming revealed a "disconnect between what the district prioritizes and what actually happens [in practice]" leading to initiative overload and fatigue (Locke et al., 2019):

> Both principals and teachers expressed the need for central office and school leadership to de-prioritize competing EBP and other initiatives more broadly and suggested that "clearly defined" school priorities around EBP and initiatives is essential to gain buy-in from teachers/staff. (p. 386)

Equity Goal: Decrease chronic absenteeism of grades K–3 students from low socioeconomic families in rural areas.

Initiative	Current Progress	Potential Impact
Attendance Policy	• Recently removed disciplinary penalties for truancy and replaced with supportive interventions • Added incentives or rewards programs to motivate strong attendance • Still need to ask families what kinds of resources they need to help improve attendance	High
Wellness Center	• Plan to deploy medical, dental, and mental health care mobile vans to rural regions • Enhance health education and information in multiple languages • Conduct basic health assessments in school (nutrition, hearing and vision tests)	High
Restorative Practices	• Adopted PBIS at the elementary level and it's working to help resolve problems that arise • The program has not been used to encourage attendance or provide support structures yet	Medium
Science Technology Engineering Art Mathematics (STEAM) Program	• Currently only offered at the district's middle schools. It may increase motivation, but is not geared toward primary age students at this time • We might consider adopting some lessons or activities in lower grades to give students a preview of the program	Low
Hybrid Schedule	• We adapted hybrid learning during the COVID-19 pandemic, but rural students' lack of access to stable internet was and continues to be a huge obstacle • We may need to consider other ways we can envision what *hybrid* means so students can receive a quality education even when not at school	Low
Anti-Bullying Curriculum	• The curriculum was purchased two years ago but has not been fully implemented yet • We need to assess whether bullying is a key factor in students not attending school • School safety and helping students stay connected are both important goals	Medium
Graduate Portrait	• The graduate portrait contains qualities and knowledge that students should attain at every level of K–12 • We should focus on the early childhood years to stress the importance of good attendance and academic success • Need to make sure that elementary teachers are equipped with curriculum and not thinking it's "a just high school thing"	Medium

Figure 2.7: Initiative correlation example.

As we examine the prioritization process in the coming sections, you will see that de-prioritizing is just as essential as giving precedence to other initiatives.

Assistant professor of doctoral leadership studies at Cardinal Stritch University Tony Frontier (2021) succinctly sums up the problem of *initiative overload*, meaning we are attempting to solve (via prioritization) a clarity paradox in which leaders assume that implementation confusion is related to a deficiency or gap to fill:

> Out of concern, [leaders] respond by adding more clutter. . . . *The problem must be that the people we serve need another program, more technical support, more emotional support, and more rewards and consequences!* None of these responses address the root cause of the problem: a lack of clarity within the system. (p. 13)

And as you've probably heard, "clarity precedes competence" (Schmoker, 2004, p. 85), so the rest of this section will help you sift through your district's various implementations to reinforce institutional alignment.

USING EQUITY FOR PRIORITIZATION

The next activity helps teams examine equity-centered initiatives their school or district is considering or has already adopted. As shown in figure 2.8 (page 50), I have updated the original rubric for prioritizing initiatives from *Leading the Launch* to remove equity as its own criterion; instead, I infuse it throughout each of the remaining criteria (Wallace, 2022). (See page 56 for a blank reproducible version of this figure). Team members each complete the rubric based on their analysis of each factor. Then the whole team compares responses and comes to consensus on to what degree the initiative is a priority. Total agreement is not necessary; the objective is to decide how to prioritize initiatives with equity squarely at the center.

The prioritization process is meant to lessen the overwhelm that can occur when attempting to juggle many complex plans. By coming to consensus on the order, timeline, and sequence, the team will be more tightly unified in its efforts, rather than inadvertently working at cross-purposes or in isolation. Stage 3 asks all involved to affirm the following mentality: "Even when I'm not closely associated with a highly prioritized project, I will lend my skills, energy, and commitment to seeing it succeed and benefit the students it is designed for." A shared pledge to reinforce institutional alignment certifies a leadership team's accomplishment of the first three stages in the implementation process.

Directions:

1. Describe the equity-centered initiative at the top of Part I.

2. In the left column, review or edit each criterion and assign a weight to its importance (sample weights can be left as is or modified).

3. Evaluate the initiative against each criterion using the guiding questions in the center column and assign a rating on the scale in the right column.

4. Multiply the weight assigned in the left column by the rating assigned in the right column.

5. Add the values together and write the total in the bottom row.

6. Repeat this process for all key initiatives in your organization before completing Part II: Initiative Prioritization Rubric.

Part I: Individual Initiative Evaluation

Equity-Centered Initiative:

Criteria and Weight	Guiding Questions	Rating Scale
Strategic Alignment Weight = 2	• To what extent is the project aligned with existing district frameworks or strategic plans *to advance equity*? • To what extent is the project aligned with the department or site's *equity-driven* vision, mission, and goals?	0 = Unsure 1 = Does not align 2 = Some alignment 3 = Full alignment
Connection to Other Initiatives Weight = 2	• To what degree does the project intersect with or support other district *equity-related* initiatives? • To what degree will the project lay a foundation to support future *equity-related* initiatives?	0 = Unsure 1 = None; stands alone 2 = Intersects; supports some 3 = Intersects; supports all
Learning Outcomes Weight = 3	• How does the data support why this initiative is needed to *mitigate performance gaps between students*? • To what extent will the project improve *equitable conditions for student learning*? • To what extent will this initiative *equitably impact students throughout the district*?	0 = Unsure 1 = Low impact 2 = Medium impact 3 = High impact

Support From Stakeholders
 	
Weight = 2
	• What is the level of *support and understanding about the need to execute this initiative to expand equity throughout the district from the following constituents?*
	
	  ◆ Students
	
	  ◆ Parents
	
	  ◆ Superintendent or senior cabinet
	
	  ◆ Governing board
	
	  ◆ Employee associations
	
	  ◆ Community
		1 = Unknown or weak level of support or understanding
		
		2 = General support and understanding
		
		3 = High level of support and understanding

Timing or Readiness Weight = 2	• What is the level of urgency of the *inequity being resolved?* • To what degree is the district ready for this initiative? • To what degree is this the right time for this initiative?	1 = Not ready; too early to tell 2 = Adequately prepared; good timing 3 = Totally prepared; perfect timing
Required Service Weight = 2	• Is the initiative required to meet legal, compliance, regulatory mandates, *or remedy racial or ethnic injustices?* • Does it fulfill a moral or ethical obligation *to disenfranchised students and families?* • Will the initiative respond to *concerns or issues raised by diverse groups* of staff, students, or parents?	1 = Not required or mandated 2 = Not required but has ethical value 3 = Required; mandated by law
Costs and Resources Weight = 2	• What are the costs and benefits of the project? • *How will we predict and measure impact on intended outcomes for underserved students?* • What are the other resources, other than money, needed to sustain *long-term improvements?*	0 = Unsure 1 = High cost, low impact 2 = Low cost, low impact 3 = High cost, high impact 4 = Low cost, high impact
Total Score		

Figure 2.8: Prioritization process.

continued ▶

Part II: Initiative Prioritization Rubric

Proposed District or School Initiatives	Total Score From Part I	Implementation Timeline
Initiative one:		☐ Immediately ☐ Within three to six months ☐ Within seven to twelve months ☐ Beyond twelve months

CONCLUSION

The initial stages are largely theoretical in nature. They are composed of collective imagination, lived experience, genuine inquiry, and anticipated outcomes. Once you have a grasp on the work that needs to be done, the team's ideas can progress from thoughts to conversations to the written word. Since inequities may not always be visible and are, indeed, often insidious, it's essential to do our best to reveal what's hidden behind the proverbial curtain before acting. Though not quite yet *real*, this three-stage set of cognitive exercises is the requisite base from which to start building the infrastructure in the trial phase, outlined in the next chapter.

Equity-Centered Problems of Practice

Equity-Centered Problem of Practice	Resources to Understand the Problem of Practice	Potential Initiatives to Address the Problem of Practice

Winding Up the Pitch Writing Exercise

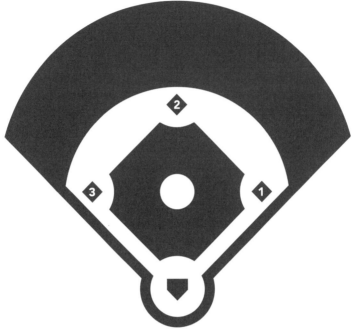

1. What is the specific initiative that I'm proposing? (A resource? A process? A program? A training? A system? A policy?)

2. What needs to be communicated, to whom, and how?

3. What are the stats (data) I need to share with the rest of the team?

4. What questions, comments, or opinions may come out of left field?

5. Why do I believe this initiative will help level the playing field for identified student groups?

Post Pitch SWOT Analysis

Directions: Summarize your impressions from the tuning protocol discussion in the four boxes.

Strengths (warm feedback; positive comments; areas of enthusiasm)	Opportunities (clarity; connections; synchronicity)
Weaknesses (cool feedback; negative comments; areas of disinterest or apathy)	Threats (disconnects; confusion; apprehensions)

Reflections
Do the strengths and opportunities to advance equity outweigh the weaknesses and threats? If not, can the balance be shifted with some adaptations?
Do I now feel more, less, or the same commitment to seeing this initiative move forward?
Does it have enough initial support from others to bring it to stage 3, prioritization?
Recommendation:

Prioritization Process

Directions:

1. Describe the equity-centered initiative at the top of Part I.

2. In the left column, review or edit each criterion and assign a weight to its importance (sample weights can be left as is or modified).

3. Evaluate the initiative against each criterion using the guiding questions in the center column and assign a rating on the scale in the right column.

4. Multiply the weight assigned in the left column by the rating assigned in the right column.

5. Add the values together and write the total in the bottom row.

6. Repeat this process for all key initiatives in your organization before completing Part II: Initiative Prioritization Rubric.

Part I: Individual Initiative Evaluation

Equity-Centered Initiative:		

Criteria and Weight	Guiding Questions	Rating Scale
Strategic Alignment Weight = 2	• To what extent is the project aligned with existing district frameworks or strategic plans *to advance equity*? • To what extent is the project aligned with the department or site's *equity-driven* vision, mission, and goals?	0 = Unsure 1 = Does not align 2 = Some alignment 3 = Full alignment
Connection to Other Initiatives Weight = 2	• To what degree does the project intersect with or support other district *equity-related* initiatives? • To what degree will the project lay a foundation to support future *equity-related* initiatives?	0 = Unsure 1 = None; stands alone 2 = Intersects; supports some 3 = Intersects; supports all
Learning Outcomes Weight = 3	• How does the data support why this initiative is needed to *mitigate performance gaps between students*? • To what extent will the project improve *equitable conditions for student learning*? • To what extent will this initiative *equitably impact students throughout the district*?	0 = Unsure 1 = Low impact 2 = Medium impact 3 = High impact

Support From Stakeholders
 	
Weight = 2
	• What is the level of *support and understanding about the need to execute this initiative to expand equity throughout the district from the following constituents*?
	
	    ♦ Students
	
	    ♦ Parents
	
	    ♦ Superintendent or senior cabinet
	
	    ♦ Governing board
	
	    ♦ Employee associations
	
	    ♦ Community
		1 = Unknown or weak level of support or understanding
		
		2 = General support and understanding
		
		3 = High level of support and understanding

Criteria and Weight	Guiding Questions	Rating Scale
Timing or Readiness Weight = 2	• What is the level of urgency of the *inequity being resolved?* • To what degree is the district ready for this initiative? • To what degree is this the right time for this initiative?	1 = Not ready; too early to tell 2 = Adequately prepared; good timing 3 = Totally prepared; perfect timing
Required Service Weight = 2	• Is the initiative required to meet legal, compliance, regulatory mandates, *or remedy racial or ethnic injustices?* • Does it fulfill a moral or ethical obligation *to disenfranchised students and families?* • Will the initiative respond to *concerns or issues raised* by *diverse groups* of staff, students, or parents?	1 = Not required or mandated 2 = Not required but has ethical value 3 = Required; mandated by law
Costs and Resources Weight = 2	• What are the costs and benefits of the project? • *How will we predict and measure impact on intended outcomes for underserved students?* • What are the other resources, other than money, needed to sustain *long-term improvements?*	0 = Unsure 1 = High cost, low impact 2 = Low cost, low impact 3 = High cost, high impact 4 = Low cost, high impact
Total Score		

Part II: Initiative Prioritization Rubric

Proposed District or School Initiatives	Total Score From Part I	Implementation Timeline
Initiative one:		☐ Immediately ☐ Within three to six months ☐ Within seven to twelve months ☐ Beyond twelve months
Initiative two:		☐ Immediately ☐ Within three to six months ☐ Within seven to twelve months ☐ Beyond twelve months
Initiative three:		☐ Immediately ☐ Within three to six months ☐ Within seven to twelve months ☐ Beyond twelve months
Initiative four:		☐ Immediately ☐ Within three to six months ☐ Within seven to twelve months ☐ Beyond twelve months
Initiative five:		☐ Immediately ☐ Within three to six months ☐ Within seven to twelve months ☐ Beyond twelve months

Trial Stages

I n the introduction, you distinguished the roadblocks in your institution and diagnosed your equity-centered problems of practice. You approached the dismantling of barriers for the identified marginalized groups in chapter 1. In chapter 2, you embarked on the hard work of research, coalition building, and prioritization. You and your team now have a clearer picture of the path forward and how to gain support to move on to the next phase of the ten-stage process. Having completed the cogni-

> ### KEY CONCEPTS
>
> **Stage 4: Experiment.** Use inquiry as a base method to test your initiative before launch.
>
> **Stage 5: Engage.** Solicit feedback on your initiative from stakeholders or peers.
>
> **Stage 6: Analyze.** Compile and interpret data about your initiative.

tive lifting in the preceding chapters, you now get to take some controlled action.

This chapter covers the three stages of the trial period: stage 4 (experiment), stage 5 (engage), and stage 6 (analyze). In stage 4, you will design one or more inquiry-based experiments to learn how your equity-centered initiative works in "real life." Real life in this case is conditional; as in any social scientific endeavor, you will intentionally select the who, what, when, where, why, and how to execute your exploratory pursuits. Once you've begun to experiment, you'll move into stage 5 and determine how people are perceiving the equity-centered initiative. After gathering this critical feedback, your team will need to decide whether to stay the course as planned, make adjustments, or in the rare case that things are going horribly wrong or causing damage, cancel the initiative. Be on high alert when experimenting with historically marginalized groups; you don't want to aggravate past injuries or escalate future ones. Both stages 4 and 5 will yield tremendous amounts of data to sift through in stage 6. You will learn some basic collection and analysis methodologies to set you up for success in your interpretation efforts. By the end of this chapter, you will have what it takes to finally decide the way forward.

STAGE 4: EXPERIMENT

Experimentation can take on different meanings to different audiences. Unfortunately, overt discrimination is not the only wrong that has been imposed on minoritized populations. Educational experimentation, often coded over the past century as *interventions*, included forcing lefties to only use their right hand to write, and using IQ tests or other standardized assessments to pigeonhole students in low-, medium-, or high-level academic tracks—not to mention flogging and paddling as a corrective disciplinary method. Perhaps we may similarly look back in fifty to one hundred years and lament the innovations we thought would revolutionize schooling in our current society. But that shouldn't stop us from pursuing progress, because we *are* improving, sometimes incrementally and sometimes by leaps and bounds. While good intentions aren't enough, they are a fine place to start.

Think back to your own childhood. What exciting discoveries did you make through play, games, or sport? How did you make friends, navigate relationships, and resolve neighborhood conflicts? In what ways did you improve upon what you learned from experience or by immersing yourself in a topic of great interest? Take a moment to remember the passions that simultaneously consumed and fueled you. Those same skills and aptitudes that naturally occupied you as a child can translate into more sophisticated approaches in your work as an equity-centered leader. The trick is tapping into the parts of yourself that remain curious, open-minded, and inventive. Suspend the inner voice that says "can't, won't, shouldn't, didn't" to fully embrace a mindset vital to constructing inventive ways to educate students who have been on the outside looking in. Open the windows. Open the door. Yank the roof off if that is what's required. Just imagine what's possible if this critical, serious work can be imbued with a spirit of hope and promise. Good. It's time to get out there.

THE ITERATIVE MODEL

Chapter 4 of *Leading the Launch* explains that synthesizing and distilling the information gathered in stages 2 and 3 will help you formulate your own equity blueprint for action (Wallace, 2022). Experimentation can take many forms. It might be conducted in a lab, through observation, or by trying a hypothesis out in the field. The driving force behind experimentation is embodied in the concept of inquiry-led professional practices.

In their book *Leading Through Spirals of Inquiry: For Equity and Quality*, Judy Halbert and Linda Kaser (2022) note, "For young people to be curious, they need to be supported and surrounded by adults who are equally curious themselves. We need to place inquiry-based approaches at the center of our own collective professional learning" (p. 18). This said, marginalized student groups must always be at the crux of the many questions you ask yourself and others throughout this stage. Halbert and Kaser's (2022) six core elements, along with the accompanying prompts, guide us closer to a focused line of inquiry. I've added in brackets the equity focus at the center of our work:

1. Scanning: What's going on for our [most disenfranchised] learners?

2. Focusing: Where are we going to focus our attention [keeping a keen eye on equity]?

3. Developing a hunch: What's leading to this [inequitable] situation and how are we contributing to [or sanctioning] it?

4. New professional learning: Where and how will we learn more about what to do [to interrupt unproductive practices and gain new competencies that increase learning outcomes for identified student groups]?

5. Taking action: What will we do differently [to improve conditions and foster diversity, inclusion, and belonging on our campuses]?

6. Checking: Have we made enough of a difference [for the students who most need it]? (Halbert & Kaser, 2022, pp. 23–26)

This spiral (hence, iterative) model is a great place to start to determine how you might design your site-based pilot to test the initiative on a limited scale and identify its merits, deficiencies, gaps, and opportunities.

PILOT STUDY

Dry run. Dress rehearsal. Scrimmage. Probation period. Field work. Research and development. These are some variations on the theme of pilot experiments. While the term *pilot study* can sound awfully formal, the operation you design doesn't have to be clinically pure or strictly adhere to scientific methodology. Whatever you decide to call it, this is the time you will spend testing out the feasibility of your fledgling equity-centered initiative. During the pilot, you hope to discover hidden costs (money and resources), handle adverse events, gain insights, and anticipate probabilities. The Regional Educational Laboratory Appalachia at SRI International's (2021) report on conducting pilot studies explains the following:

> A pilot study is useful when stakeholders want to understand how well an initiative integrates into existing infrastructure and programming to make decisions about whether to continue or possibly expand its use. By pilot-testing on a small scale, decision makers can identify what modifications, conditions, and supports are necessary for implementing the initiative on a larger scale. (p. 2)

Since the point of piloting is to determine whether something can be replicated or expanded in future settings, the team should make a list of possible sites with the costs and benefits of each prior to choosing one. As they say in the real estate business, location, location, location! Selecting the appropriate environment for your pilot is key.

Keep your equity lens at the forefront when considering options. Though some places may seem easier (for example, a highly effective principal, convenient proximity to wraparound services, enthusiastic teachers, and diverse student population), you must balance out the tendency to take the easier path with the fact that you will also need to reproduce this later in other contexts that likely won't be as ideal. Each option has its pros and cons, but those can be better anticipated when engaging in the planning template activity. The scenario that follows represents a precursor to the actual selection process.

Consider the following scenario as it is applied to the spiral of inquiry. If our purpose is to develop a multipronged approach to bolstering early literacy skills for kindergartners who test below English language arts standards, the following sample of the six core elements provides some baseline answers and predictions.

1. **Scanning:** What's going on for our most disenfranchised learners?

   Students attending different schools in the district are exhibiting different competencies and progress toward literacy. Our north-end schools seem to be falling behind the ones in the south in meeting literacy benchmarks. The neighborhood demographics suggest that the high concentrations of English learners in the north may be a factor.

2. **Focusing:** Where are we going to focus our attention, keeping a keen eye on equity?

There are two north-end schools with similar student populations but different outcomes in literacy assessments. We might focus on both to see how the literacy program we've chosen can and will address the needs of a range of English learners to assess whether they are receiving equitable services.

3. **Developing a hunch:** What's leading to this inequitable situation, and how are we contributing to or sanctioning it?

    Of the two schools, one has a principal with significant early literacy teaching experience and explicit goals, training, and expectations for her teachers. The other school's principal has been more focused on science and mathematics. By not providing a clear and unified district direction, we have been leaving site leaders to decide what's important on their own. We need to consider the predispositions of our administrators across the district to ensure that they all have the requisite training to support English learners.

4. **New professional learning:** Where and how will we learn more about what to do to interrupt unproductive practices and gain new competencies that increase learning outcomes for identified student groups?

    We could start by conducting the pilot at both sites, providing both principals with the guidance and support they need to implement it for four months. We will provide leadership coaching, professional development on cultural competency, and support from the district's English language acquisition department. After that period, we will assess the students to gauge levels of progress.

5. **Taking action:** What will we do differently to improve conditions and foster diversity, inclusion, and belonging on our campuses?

    If this program results in literacy growth across the board, we will either expand the pilot to three other sites for another six months or possibly implement it across the entire district. In addition, we will conduct pre-and post-interviews with students to find out if they are feeling more included and successful at school.

6. **Checking:** Have we made enough of a difference for the students who most need it?

At the end of the ten-month two-pilot cycle, we will review all districtwide data to determine whether to adopt the program, make adjustments, or look for another way to meet the needs of students struggling to acquire English literacy competencies.

The spiral of inquiry is a brief version of the feasibility measure exercise that follows. It's meant to help leaders make initial high-level suppositions about what the pilot might entail. But the proof in the pudding, so to speak, will come from delving into how practical it will be to pull off the pilot based on participant qualities, willingness, and cooperation.

VERIFYING FEASIBILITY OF THE PILOT

The National Center for Complementary and Integrative Health (n.d.) offers a simple checklist that can help experimenters discern whether their pilot ideas are practical or not by addressing certain feasibility questions and responding with potential metrics. The topic for these guidelines is related to developing and testing mind and body interventions in health care. Since these components pertain to a different field, I've made some adaptations that better apply to education in figure 3.1. (See page 93 for a blank reproducible version of this figure.)

After determining and meeting your feasibility thresholds, you should be ready for the main event. Here are some additional tenets for your team to monitor prior to commencing your equity-centered pilot.

- We all have values, beliefs, and assumptions that we must examine, name, and challenge when crafting an inquiry-based pilot to support systemically marginalized and historically underserved students.

- We need a diverse variety of skills, resources, perspectives, voices, and capabilities to implement an inquiry-based pilot.

- We must seek valuable ways to involve students and families in the pilot design.

- We must authentically enlist teaching and support staff in the formulation, delivery, and assessment of the pilot.

- Pilots are meant to be experimental. We will keep open minds and hearts and persist throughout the process, even when it gets hard.

Having delved into the inquiry process at a high level, your team can now begin formulating the details needed to plan your pilot. To demonstrate how this might work, here's an example from a district that wants to centralize human resources processes related to staffing for special education students. In the current

Feasibility Questions	Feasibility Measures
Who is my target population and how can I encourage them to participate?	• Requisite number enlisted in the pilot for the duration • Average time from invitation to acceptance, agreement, or commitment
Are there benefits to randomizing the target population or are preexisting groups sufficient (or preferable)?	• Availability of preexisting classes, teams, or departments willing to participate • Proportion of eligible candidates who participate • Proportion of enrolled who stay in the pilot for more than (desired number) sessions, months, meetings, appointments, and so on
Will I be able to keep participants in the study?	• Retention rates for study measures (number that must remain for validity's sake) • Anticipated minimum dropout rate acceptable
Will participants do what they are asked to do?	• Adherence rates to study protocols or parameters • Fidelity to which participants implement the initiative as designed
Are the activities or assessments too burdensome?	• Proportion of planned assessments that need to be completed • Percentage of activities (such as lessons, trainings, exercises, tasks, or services) executed or performed throughout
Are the conditions acceptable to participants?	• Amount of support or training required • Quantity and quality of necessary materials • Satisfaction ratings (pre-, mid-, and post-trial period)
Are the conditions credible?	• Expectation of benefits to targeted groups • Appropriateness of setting or environment • Degree of replicability beyond the pilot

Figure 3.1: Adapted National Center for Complementary and Integrative Health (n.d.) feasibility measures for educational pilots.

model, principals at each site are responsible for hiring their own special education professionals, including paraeducators, teachers, behavior specialists, and school psychologists, just as they do the rest of their general education staff. It's widely known that special educators are in short supply, not only in their state or province but also nationally. This results in severe inequities, not to mention compliance risks or legal liabilities, between campuses.

As the arrangement stands, which school gets the most competent special education staff comes down to luck, resulting in an inability to recruit qualified employees at every location where they're needed. In addition, students' diverse disabilities are not equally distributed across the system, which makes recruitment that much more challenging; some sites have a greater proportion of students with autism or cognitive delays or low-incidence conditions such as sight or hearing impairments. Yet principals lack the budget or other means to adequately staff for these specialized needs. The special education director examines the problem, pitches a plan, obtains high prioritization, and gets the go-ahead to pilot a centralized staffing program at two of the district's eight elementary schools, as shown in the example in figure 3.2. (See page 95 for a blank reproducible version of this figure.)

Piloting is only one approach to experimenting with your budding initiative. You will certainly gather plenty of valuable information about how the trial is going during and after its completion. You should also think about other ways to gather intel during stage 4, such as the following.

- Perform unannounced and unscheduled observations to calibrate your understanding, seek out patterns, and draw conclusions about how equity is being advanced at the site (even when no one is watching).

- Conduct field visits to the location to perceive whether the climate, culture, and energy surrounding the project is enhancing marginalized individuals' experiences on campus.

- Engage in informal person-on-the-street interviews with program participants.

- Spend a day or more shadowing a student who is at the focus of the intervention or a teacher who is testing out the new material.

- Run an ethnographic fly-on-the-wall study to gain insights into how the study subjects are interacting with their revamped environment.

- Participate short term in the pilot yourself (if appropriate) or spend time with a demonstration or simulated model of the activity to experience the viewpoints of your intended student groups.

Or you can combine any of the preceding strategies to learn as much as you can about how the trial stage is going. By diversifying your attempts, the evidence you gather can help confirm initial findings or reveal discrepancies that need further evaluation.

Directions: Use this planning template with your leadership team to prepare for your equity-centered initiative pilot. Fill out the right column individually or as a team with the goal of coming to consensus.

Critical Questions	Responses
1. What is the scope (and what are the limitations) of the pilot?	**The pilot will take place at [locations] for [amount of time]:** Caldwell Elementary School and Mercer Elementary School March through August for hiring and placement; September through January for implementation **We selected these locations and circumstances for the following equity-related reasons:** Twelve percent of Caldwell students have IEPs, including three students who are deaf or hard of hearing, nine on the autism spectrum, fourteen who require speech and language services, and twenty-three with specific learning disabilities. Eleven percent of Mercer students have IEPs, including two students with orthopedic impairments, four with emotional disabilities, seven with ADHD, and nineteen with specific learning disabilities. Caldwell and Mercer are 2.2 miles apart with similar racial and socioeconomic demographics. Thirty-six and 41 percent receive free and reduced lunch, respectively, and both schools are approximately one-quarter each Asian, Black, Hispanic, and White. The rest of the district has similar racial demographics, and has 30 percent students from low-income households. These sites were selected for proximity to each another and because they are the highest-needs and lowest-achieving schools related to their special education population's standardized assessment scores as well as lack of legal compliance concerning students' inadequate progress toward meeting their IEP goals.
2. What do we want to learn through conducting this pilot?	**Our equity-centered goals and intentions behind this pilot are:** To remedy the disparity between district schools' ability to serve special education students by revising staffing procedures and changing to a centralized model, which will result in improved outcomes for disabled students. **We hope to discover:** That having the special education department take over the duties of recruiting, screening, hiring, and placing highly qualified and appropriate staff at the two sites will improve student academic, social-emotional, and behavioral outcomes, aid progress toward IEP goals, and generate more supportive inclusion opportunities in general education classrooms.

continued ▶

Figure 3.2: Example pilot planning template.

Critical Questions	Responses
3. How will we know if we've learned what we need from the pilot?	**We will use the following formative tools to collect data on the intended student groups' progress:** • Special education parent feedback meetings • General education staff surveys • Student observations during instruction and unscheduled time • Principal interviews • Special education team focus groups • Midyear review of IEPs in January following the staffing pilot in the fall **We will analyze and interpret the data using these methods:** Qualitative analysis—Disaggregate and interpret staff surveys; solicit Likert scale responses from highly dissatisfied to highly satisfied; compute and evaluate number of students making at least 20 percent increased progress toward IEP goals Quantitative analysis—Watch and dissect video and audio recordings from parent meetings and staff focus groups; review and ccde transcripts from principal interviews and student observations
4. What will we do to intervene when or if it's not going well?	**We will look for these indicators that interventions or adaptations may be needed to better support underserved students' learning goals:** • Formal and informal feedback from stakeholders (parents, students, staff) that indicate problems or dissatisfaction with specific components of the pilot • Check-ins with new hires that suggest mismatches in placement, insufficient preparation, or obstacles to executing their job duties effectively • Students failing to thrive or make progress as reported during their annual IEP meetings (for those which occur during the pilot period) • Above typical change of placement requests made by parents or teachers • Increased disciplinary referrals, failing grades, poor attendance, lack of motivation, or other indicators of student disengagement **Our intervention plan will include these possible strategies:** • Adjust programming or services based on stakeholder input • Provide coaching, mentorship, or professional development for staff who need it • Convene additional IEP meetings to recalibrate goals, strategies, or interventions • Embed extra collaboration and observation time in the schedule for general and special education staff to align expectations and fine-tune instruction and other supports • Reassign or exchange staff caseloads between or within pilot sites, when appropriate • Reassign students to alternative staff members, when appropriate

| 5. What will we do to expand on early successes? | **We will look for these indicators that we are exceeding our original goals:** |
| | |

We will look for these indicators that we are exceeding our original goals:

- Formal and informal positive feedback from students, families, and staff
- Observations that students are engaging and thriving inside and outside instructional settings
- Students meeting and exceeding their learning, social-emotional, and behavioral goals
- Staff reports of high satisfaction with the new model and their assignments
- Non-pilot site principals and teachers requesting to have the centralized staffing formula introduced to their own campuses

Our expansion plans will include these possible strategies:

- Expand the pilot in the second semester to one or two additional campuses
- Consider adding innovations, technologies, or other research-based enhancements to the pilot to keep momentum trending upward
- Work with human resources to start planning the following year for recruitment and retention of hard to fill special education positions
- Hold a showcase to celebrate the successes at Caldwell and Mercer to generate enthusiasm, build community, and foster parent support at non-pilot sites

---

6. How will we determine whether to terminate, continue, or expand the pilot?

After running the pilot for six months and collecting feedback, analyzing data, and drawing conclusions, we will meet on January 30 to determine next steps.

Our decision making will include the following equity-based thresholds or metrics:

- An end-of-pilot comprehensive survey of parents, students, and staff involved in the study that shows stakeholder satisfaction rates of over 75 percent
- Skills gains in over 60 percent of students with IEPs
- Increased rates of attendance by 10 percent or more
- Decrease of disciplinary referrals or consequences by 15 percent or more
- Influx of intra-district transfer requests from teachers and students into Caldwell or Mercer
- Reduction in lawsuits or civil rights complaints

Additional considerations:

Making this initiative successful beyond the pilot period significantly depends on recruiting and retaining high-quality staff. We should consider how to promote our innovative spirit outside the district to increase awareness at universities and other preparation programs and to attract the best candidates starting in February.

STAGE 5: ENGAGE

If you're not careful, the concept of *stakeholder engagement* can verge on being perfunctory, something you have to do and check off the list to move on to the next stage. To be genuine, communication must flow two ways. It's not enough to hold a community meeting, send out a survey, or listen to public comment at a board meeting. Crafted well, the responses from each engagement opportunity can serve as a beacon and a barometer. When practicing engagement with an equity lens, we seek to hear voices not typically represented through the usual channels. As education activist bell hooks (1994) proclaims, "To hear each other is an exercise in recognition" (p. 41). Racial and linguistic affinity groups, neighborhood councils, and other grassroots organizations or informal community leaders should be tapped to cohost opportunities in ways that will make people feel most comfortable and free to share their ideas and concerns. Building ongoing relationships with families and communities also develops enduring trust and social capital.

Jess L. Gregory (2017) proposes the following:

> Today, leadership responsibilities in schools are shared more now than in the past. Beyond simply being shared, educational leadership can be redefined as such that every individual in a school has the capacity to be a leader in a given situation. When leadership is approached this way, then every member of the school community is responsible for shaping the school's culture and, to some degree, participates in relationships that demonstrate imbalances of power. (p. 143)

Under this framework, we take turns being leader and follower, facilitator and participant, and expert and novice. Experiencing an array of functions builds empathy and understanding and fosters creativity and resourcefulness.

As such, we must rethink what we know about traditional forms of engagement. For example, it is common for people attending an outreach session to be asked their name, where they work, where they live, or their occupation. This seemingly innocuous attempt at getting to know each other may inadvertently generate a sort of social ranking system in the room—those with professional titles, influential jobs, or who possess namesakes of prominent community members can establish a pecking order that threatens your equity-centered intentions from the start.

To counter this, facilitators leading the event may choose to introduce themselves with their name and title to help orient the group to their own role (referring to a principal, department chair, or fiscal services director), but then say, "We're all going to go by first names here if that's OK with everyone. We're all on equal ground." Kirstin Moreno and Xiaomei Song (2021) also underscore the need to recognize the following:

> There may be complex power dynamics among the various stake-holders you engage. Power dynamics can be influenced by identities, hierarchies, previous interactions, competing goals, and structural inequities. It is essential to create an environment in which power differentials are limited to the extent possible. (p. 8)

Thus, a large part of leading for equity includes recognizing, naming, and actively upending conventional power structures. Leaders will be pleased to find that this new mode of operation flings open the doors to creative solutions, innovative ideas, and ingenious inventions. Another way of looking at this is explained by action-researcher Jacob W. Neumann (2018):

> Power is not a single, fixed thing that only certain people can possess, and we know that it moves in multiple directions at once and not just in linear fashion. Thus, instead of describing it as something that flows, like a river, it's more helpful to think of power relations as forming a web. And as various people within a social, professional, or other kind of network exert power on each other, they all help to spin that web , making the connections more "dense." (p. 33)

Reconsider von Uexküll's (2010) definition of *umwelt*, shared in chapter 1 (page 11): "Every subject spins out, like the spider's threads, its relations to certain qualities of things and weaves them into a solid web, which carries its existence" (p. 53). In this case, the web is not the individual's creation, but one that the group weaves together. This unique way of reframing power can distribute it more evenly throughout the system. And if you've ever tried to pull down a majestically woven spider web, you know that its architecture does not give way to human hands as easily as you'd imagine!

THE Cs OF COMMUNICATION

Referring to the Cs of Communication from *Leading the Launch* can help round out your approach (Wallace, 2022). As in the original version, communication is always a two-way street. Rather than speaking *at* people, we connect *with* people by both openly affirming our aspirations and listening to others' viewpoints while integrating their ideas into our planning. Research from New Zealand, which can be universalized across the globe, underscores that:

> Families' cultural background influences to some degree the nature of partnership, and lower involvement in school activities tends to be related to minority cultural backgrounds and lower socioeconomic status. When schools find out about, acknowledge and utilise families' community knowledge and practices, it can help to minimise the challenges in developing effective partnerships where there are differences between the home and school environments. (Hargraves, 2019)

Trust is fragile; it can be built or demolished by words, tone, and vocabulary, especially when interacting with people who've experienced systemic oppression, discrimination, or racism. Your mere presence as a representative of an institution that might evoke dreadful memories can pose a hurdle to jump before you even open your mouth. But you are not expected to know everything about someone else's culture, and worrying about saying the wrong thing doesn't need to be stultifying. Assuming an inquisitive posture, being personally vulnerable, and asking to be corrected if you misspeak can lower anxiety for both parties and establish a foundation from which to start.

The Cs of Communication are really about empathy and rapport. Sharing our humanness through words, actions, body language, discourse, and other means of expression is a gift we have at our disposal, and one that can wondrously kindle communion and community between disparate people. Therefore, take some time to decide which method or combination of outreach strategies is most appropriate to reach your target audiences with an inclusive equity stance in mind, as modeled in table 3.1.

The strategies you select should be associated with the circumstances. For instance, if the initiative has some negative buzz or misinformation, you may want to pair Check-In and Circulate to soothe people's minds while correcting the record. If the initiative is technically difficult to explain, you could use Correlate and Calibrate to ensure better understanding. If the topic is sensitive or controversial in nature, you might want to Collaborate and Consult to assure participants feel their voices are being heard. Whatever you do, just keep communicating by trying out different approaches to introduce and infuse your initiative into the public arena.

In addition to selecting appropriate tools for the occasion, you may want to consider varying extents that you will communicate with different stakeholders. Recalling Murphy's (2015) advice cited in stage 2 (page 40), you want to concentrate your energy in the directions that will yield the greatest impact. Squandering

Table 3.1: The Cs of Communication

Cs of Communications Methods	Inclusive Equity Stance
Correspond: Send out messages, emails, flyers, or newsletters to inform stakeholders about initiative details, meeting dates and times, or next steps.	• Translate materials into all major languages. • Use simple, plain, understandable terms. • Make sure all details are included in a single place. • Add landmarks, maps, or images to accommodate all literacy levels.
Collaborate: Brainstorm ideas, novel approaches, or problem-solving techniques with team members.	• Ask for input. • Notice who has not shared and present them with nonthreatening opportunities to do so. • Explain how you are going to use the input you receive. • Solicit possible community resources that the group may know about. • Whenever possible, involve leaders or facilitators who represent diverse backgrounds.
Come to Consensus: Distill ideas from the think tank and agree on the best ones.	• Collect all ideas without judgment. • Invite individuals to privately narrow down to their top three choices. • Create a process to choose from the most popular ideas with the whole group.
Contribute: Solicit data, information, and suggestions for improving the pilot phase.	• Introduce the session with the intention to hear honest and experiential feedback. • Share information gathered to date. • Have a virtual and physical suggestion box for anonymous feedback.
Consult: Find experts in the field on the topic to share insights, professional opinions, and guidance on moving the initiative forward.	• Bring in respected experts from the community to present or answer questions that reflect the audience's racial, ethnic, linguistic, or cultural backgrounds. • Use materials, research, and images that physically resemble the community.
Correlate: Explicitly link the initiative to work already being done at the district or site so people can connect the dots.	• Make a chart of district or site plans that show the connections between initiatives. • Create a timeline of past initiatives that have led to this point. • State exactly how this initiative is meant to increase equitable outcomes.
Compromise: Make concessions for what's not working and change up the original strategy to remove unnecessary stumbling blocks.	• Describe what's going well and what needs improvement. • Request input from their own or their children's experiences with the pilot period. • Troubleshoot solutions to change the strategy going forward.

continued ▲

Cs of Communications Methods	Inclusive Equity Stance
Calibrate: Bring external factors into account or compare with other data, then make corrections as needed.	• Acknowledge changing or emerging conditions affecting the initiative. • Seek clarity on what might be adjusted for improvements.
Check-In: Visit, touch base, inquire, poll, survey, dialogue, take the temperature, and observe what's going on using all of the faculties at your disposal.	• Drop in at cultural, religious, or social events or celebrations in the community for informal chats. • Spend time with people before and after the outreach session to hear additional concerns or ideas for consideration. • Bring translators whenever appropriate.
Confess: Concede to any errors in judgment or execution along the way, whether made inadvertently or not.	• Openly share challenges faced in the trial period. • Say how you plan to make improvements or course corrections. • Float ideas with the group and see what resonates.
Commit: Pledge resources, support, or whatever else is needed to promote the project's long-term success.	• Explain high-level funding sources to support the initiative now and in the future. • Talk about how the personnel, resources, and implementation rollout will take place. • Assure the community that the program will be supported for the long term.
Circulate: Share widely between and beyond stakeholder groups to publicize the initiative. Blanket the site or district with information via social media, sound bites, and word of mouth to expand outreach.	• Use social media to share short blurbs on aspects of the initiative and hallmarks along the way. • Find allies and influencers in each community to help spread the messages and vouch for the initiative's credibility. • Start (good) rumors about positive impacts via formal and informal multilingual media channels and outlets.
Conclude: Once input has been gathered, summarize the responses, agreements, and action steps, and circle back to those who participated in the outreach.	• Keep in touch with stakeholders who've championed as well as challenged the cause to demonstrate that diverse perspectives are valued. • Create a calendar or schedule for keeping the initiative on people's radar. • Hold celebrations or ceremonies to honor achievements related to the program.
Carry-Through: Keep promises.	• Say what you mean and mean what you say (as in, don't be disingenuous).

Source: Adapted from Wallace, 2022.

precious time on the naysayers or neglecting your natural allies will not forward your cause to large degree.

Figure 3.3 is a spectrum to help consider how much to invest in three dimensions of a school or district community. (See page 97 for a blank reproducible version of this figure.) On the right side of the spectrum, *organizers* are the people who should be nurtured the most as they will stand up as evangelists and advocates of the equity-centered initiative and lend it credence in their spheres of influence. While *obstructors* on the opposite end of the spectrum may have a high level of influence, their diminished interest in change efforts can be neutralized. By not giving them a public platform to debate the merits of the plan, you can minimize their impact. Not to be dismissed, *observers* need differentiated attention as well. Though their personal investment may not be as high, their status as metaphorical satellites can help the planets come together into alignment.

Figure 3.3: Continuum of stakeholder groups.

CASE STUDY

Consider this scenario of an initiative meant to address the disproportionate number of post-pandemic third grade boys elected for grade retention due to perceived social immaturity paired with slow literacy acquisition. The site principal is concerned with the higher than typical number of referrals stemming from the third-grade teaching team (in allegiance with the fourth-grade team) to hold back boys of all demographics at increasing rates—particularly since, according to the Education Trust–West, "Grade retention disproportionately affects Black, Latino, and Native students and English learners. . . . Students who are held back experience negative academic, social, and emotional outcomes over time" (Davis, 2021). The principal proposes a plan to host a single-gender summer "boot camp" to bolster the boys' academic skills and behavioral self-management plus boost their self-esteem and attitudes toward school before they matriculate to fourth grade. In addition to the curriculum, the boys will engage in fun, social activities that cater to their psychological and physical growth.

The interest groups include the following constituents, peppered throughout each of the three dimensions: parents of children being recommended for retention; non-affected caregivers of students in third and fourth grades; teachers at all grade levels; non-instructional school staff; and the extended school community. The obstructors want the students to repeat third grade; the organizers will champion for the students to pass on to fourth grade; and the observers will wait to see if this might spread to students in other grades going forward. Thus, the principal must present valid and compelling research on the lifelong detrimental effects of retention on young males, including ties to the "school to prison pipeline"—which posits that "Across the U.S., 85 percent of juveniles who interact with the court system are functionally illiterate, and 60 percent of the nation's inmates are illiterate" (Zoukis, 2017)—to convince the various stakeholders to get onboard with this special intervention.

MASLOW'S HIERARCHY FOR FAMILY ENGAGEMENT

Once you've identified the varying levels of investment and interest in the initiative, the next activity digs even deeper into your audience's consciousness to prepare for hosting a successful community engagement event. In *Leading the Launch*, I explain the following:

> By applying the theory of Abraham Maslow's (1943, 1954) hierarchy of human needs to your toolkit, you can deliberately accommodate diverse needs as well as break down the barriers that can keep a wider variety of people from showing up. In his research, Maslow developed a hierarchy, usually presented as a pyramid, with the most basic needs at the bottom: (1) physiological, (2) safety, (3) belonging, and (4) esteem. Individuals must meet these first four needs before moving on to the final one, which relates to personal growth: (5) self-actualization. (Wallace, 2022, p. 73)

Figure 3.4 encourages planning teams to attend to the audience's composite needs to lower the anxiety of participants during the outreach activity. (See page 98 for a reproducible version of this figure.)

EQUITABLE STAKEHOLDER ENGAGEMENT

Figure 3.4 may have sparked some questions on your team as to how to access relevant resources to meet the diverse needs of your audience. If your district has a student services department or community outreach division, they likely hold key information about local, state, and national organizations that connect families with language translation services, health and human services, childcare, and transit options. If this knowledge base doesn't exist in-house, the internet can fill

Directions: The left column contains each of Maslow's (1943, 1954) categories along with a key tenet describing the need. The middle column offers suggestions for leadership teams to contemplate and plan for outreach with a focus on equity. The right column is designed for leadership teams to add specific details for their own locales regarding each level on the hierarchy.

Maslow's Hierarchy of Needs	Guiding Questions for Equity-Centered Family and Community Engagement	Team Planning Notes for Engagement Sessions
Level 5: Self-Actualization Tenet: Achieving Potential or Mastery	What is the purpose of the outreach? How can we deliver on participants' expectations? What kinds of active roles can we give participants? How might we personalize the experience? What kinds of expertise or professional experience can be tapped from people in the room? What is the problem we are trying to solve? How can we utilize collective knowledge and skill sets? What types of high-level critical thinking tasks should we employ?	
Level 4: Self-Esteem Tenet: Acceptance	How can we honor all cultures, languages, and background experiences in the room? What are some mechanisms we might use to validate suggestions? How should we differentiate instruction for a range of participants? How might we offer appreciation or encouragement to open discussion? How will we let people know that we respect their involvement by setting and committing to norms? When and how will we check for understanding using the audience's native languages?	
Level 3: Love and Belonging Tenet: Relationships	Who will we ask to make personalized invitations or phone calls? Who will coordinate the volunteers to guide people from the parking lot to the meeting space? Who will design and post multilingual welcome and directional signs and greet participants at the door? How might we arrange tables and chairs to boost interactions? What kinds of nonthreatening icebreakers might help build a feeling of community? How might the facilitator use an anecdote or personal story to set the tone? What different cultures are in the room and how might those participants best respond to engaging in group activities? How can we encourage work in collaborative teams?	

continued ▶

Figure 3.4: Engagement strategies.

Maslow's Hierarchy of Needs	Guiding Questions for Equity-Centered Family and Community Engagement	Team Planning Notes for Engagement Sessions
Level 2: Safety Tenet: Comfort	Who will be responsible for monitoring the heat or air conditioning to moderate temperatures? What are the most convenient and centralized locations for maximum participation? How will we ensure accessibility for people with disabilities? How will we address unintentional stereotyping or bias from others? What are some other kinds of comforts we can provide?	
Level 1: Physiological Well-Being Tenet: Food, Shelter, Health	Who will coordinate and provide on-site childcare during the meeting? What kinds of snacks or meals should we have available that are considerate of religious and cultural principles (such as vegetarianism, veganism, Kosher, Halal, and so on)? How can we extend transportation options (for example, transit maps, tickets, free parking)? What kinds of arrangements do we need to make for inclement weather? What are some places we can leverage that are meaningful to the community (for example, community center, apartment complex courtyard, religious institutions)? How will we stagger meeting times to accommodate caregivers' various work and home schedules? Are there any appropriate takeaways or door prizes we can offer?	

Source: Adapted from Maslow, 1943, 1954.

many gaps; but also think about your high school–aged students and whether and how they can be called on as a volunteer workforce during outreach sessions. They know the lay of the land, both in their own neighborhoods and on campus, so they can be the ideal ambassadors.

There are many other creative and practical ways to engage families as you enact equity-centered initiatives in your organization. Here are some ideas to add to your toolkit.

- Consider hiring a full-time family liaison at the site or district level, one whose job is 100 percent dedicated to outreach and support for families in your community.

- Establish a practice of doing home visits.

- Set an expectation for yourself and your staff to regularly attend neighborhood events and social activities.

- Seek out individuals in your schools who can serve as cultural brokers and can build bridges with diverse groups.

- Forge alliances with valued community, religious, and political leaders.

- Learn the lingo, or at least try to pick up a few words or phrases in the major languages other than English in your region; your attempts will show your willingness to be vulnerable and step into their shoes as learners.

- Show authentic interest and nonjudgmental curiosity about others' life experiences.

- Share stories of your own personal challenges and offer words of encouragement about perseverance (while being conscious of not appearing dismissive or deficit-minded regarding other people's hardships).

Though stakeholder engagement is called out as a singular stage in the process, it really should permeate the nine other stages to leadership team–determined degrees. People want to know that their perspectives, experiences, and opinions matter and have been considered as the initiative evolves from conception to launch. This is exceedingly important when implementing equity-centered initiatives for historically marginalized communities. Sometimes past injustices or injuries can color perceptions or induce reluctance to attend school-sponsored events. It's our job to clear the way forward with honesty, reliability, and consistency.

STAGE 6: ANALYZE

"Without data, you're just another person with an opinion" is a famous quotation attributed to mid-20th century statistician W. Edwards Deming, though unconfirmed by any verifiable source material, or, ironically, hard data. Though the terms may change from time to time, "data-informed," "data-directed," or "data-driven" decision making is nothing new in the field of education. However, there is sometimes a *knowing-doing gap* when it comes to collecting and applying the wealth of information we gathered in the previous five stages of the new initiative process. The knowing-doing gap occurs when there is a disconnect between knowledge and action (Pfeffer & Sutton, 2000), which can be calamitous when implementing equity-centered programming.

Educators may realize that data are important and multiple inputs are needed to validate conclusions, but we don't always take the time or expend the energy to dig deeply into what the numbers or words are telling us. How can a problem of practice be defined, much less remedied, if there is little evidence to back it up; or if the evidence is abundant but disregarded? You don't want to have come this far only to execute a *solution looking for a problem* when there are plenty of real and urgent issues related to equity in schools. Rest assured; you already have what it takes to carry out the next part of the mission.

In *Leading the Launch*, chapter 6 introduced you to two methods of data collection: surveys and focus groups (Wallace, 2022). Both are sound ways to collect essential clues to monitor how your initiative is doing. Between those tools and the mammoth amount of qualitative and quantitative data you gathered during stages 4 and 5 of this process, you are certainly ready to start making meaning. But to really get at the heart of being equity centered, before we delve into the analysis process, here's one more activity to try that combines stages 4–6.

ASSET-BASED COMMUNITY MAPPING

Similar to the knowing-doing gap, it's one thing to know *about* your community and another to *know* your community. Not all educators live among their students, for myriad reasons; some may live in the same town but in different neighborhoods, while many commute from other areas or regions. There's no judgment about where you reside, but if it's not close to your district's families, visiting their neighborhoods is an invaluable way to form deeper connections. Seeing where they gather, where they shop, where they worship, and where they conduct their personal and professional business provides priceless insights into the microcosm from which your students emerge before they arrive at your school each morning.

Thus, asset-based community mapping is an exceptional way to both forge those crucial relationships as well as amass and contextualize key data. The theory of action behind this approach is to identify the formal and informal resources that a community holds, values, and exhibits by spending quality time in your district's neighborhoods. Community mapping can be conducted innumerable ways, and you can always add other strategies to fortify your efforts and enrich the experience. Be respectful. Be humble. Be curious. The only other hard and fast rule is to not forget to involve students to represent the territory! Follow these steps to conduct effective asset-based community mapping.

1. Using data from your student information system or other online databases, select an area of the district to map based on demographics, assessment data, attendance rates, or any other pertinent criteria.

2. Select the data you want to collect and develop tools to accurately do so; since your goals are related to advancing equity, carefully consider what to ask or look for.

3. Physically go out into the community to interview residents and attend community meetings, events, or social activities. Also, just go to hang out, meet people on the street, and walk the block to heighten your observational awareness.

4. Examine the data to compose an initial impression. See where there are key missing pieces of information and go back out to discover more.

5. Communicate your findings to the community, get its feedback to ensure accuracy, and revise your report. Remember that this is an asset-based approach so screen your language carefully to avoid deficit thinking and unconscious bias.

6. Set priorities and make recommendations to the school board and other decision makers.

7. Take action!

The good news is that you don't have to reinvent the wheel. Other organizations have already developed highly effective tools for community mapping that you can access online. Your first stop should be the University of California Los Angeles (UCLA) Department of Psychology's School Mental Health Project (www.smhp.psych.ucla.edu), which has compiled a comprehensive technical aid packet titled Resource Mapping and Management to Address Barriers to Learning: An Intervention for Systemic Change. It contains dozens of practical resources for educators and can be accessed at (shorturl.at/bqILZ). Digital Promise (2018) also published a user-friendly guide to asset mapping with a customizable template and list of handy online materials to guide educators through identifying education innovation clusters to "uncover creative solutions to local challenges, elevate the voices and talents of marginalized community members, and build new connections within a region" (p. 3). The guide can be accessed at (https://digitalpromise.org/wp-content/uploads/2018/09/asset-mapping.pdf). You might adopt an already existing resource or pick and choose from an assortment of options to customize your own outreach efforts. I could go on with other approaches, but you now have more than enough to work with. Once you've hit your data accumulation targets, the next step is discovering what it all means.

QUANTITATIVE DATA ANALYSIS

Unless you have a dedicated department in your district or affiliation with a nearby higher-learning institution to run your data through sophisticated software programs and provide detailed reports, your own data analysis process will likely be more rudimentary. Since it's not a practical expectation that most schools and districts have access to such a high level of expertise, there are a few simple yet powerful approaches we can employ without much training. This is not to say, however, that it will be any less meaningful or actionable than using advanced methodologies—it just may not be publishable in a peer-reviewed educational journal anytime soon. In the next section, we will look at the main components of quantitative and qualitative data analysis.

Thankfully, there are myriad resources to make quantitative analysis more accessible and user-friendly. In the aptly titled and reasonably short five-page publication, *A Really Simple Guide to Quantitative Data Analysis*, Peter Samuels (2020) proffers a twelve-step process to help budding researchers interpret the findings they've compiled. Note that this process only applies to the numerical or quantifiable information you've collected. Because the first five steps of Samuels's twelve-step process for research analysis apply to descriptive analysis and the remaining seven get into statistical testing, we will only use the following first five for our purposes (Samuels, 2020).

1. **Start with an aim and research questions:** This step ensures you set a focus for the investigation to avoid vague or unstructured research gathering. It is possible to find research that seems significant but is only a random event; developing specific questions about your focus will help avoid such discoveries.

2. **Collect data consistent with your aim and research questions:** This step helps organize your data collection efforts. Ask yourself where you will collect the data (your sample), how much data you should gather, and how you will conduct the data collection process.

3. **Process your data and create a raw data spreadsheet:** In conjunction with step 2, this step helps organize the data you do collect. Create a spreadsheet for your data, with types of data distinguished in the columns and any significant instances of data in the rows.

4. **Get a feel for your data with a descriptive analysis:** Interpret your data by representing it visually and in written form. Create purposeful charts, tables, and summaries from the raw data. Compare variables in these new formats. What best explains your question to your reader? This is where you decide the shape your data will take when you generate your reports.

5. **Interpret and report on your analysis informally:** After completing the previous four steps, you are ready to generate a narrative to accompany your data analysis. Answer your research questions by informally interpreting your descriptive statistics.

We covered Samuels's (2020) steps 1 and 2 in stage 4 of the *Leading the Launch* protocol: (1) start with an aim and research questions and (2) collect data consistent with your aim and research questions (Wallace, 2022). These are both related to the inquiry process you conducted as a pilot or other experiment out in the field.

The next steps are (3) process your data and create a raw data spreadsheet and (4) get a feel for your data with a descriptive analysis. Step 3 means that your data must be downloaded from its original source, such as an online survey or observation tracking form, into a spreadsheet-type format. Very often, the data will not arrive as clean or orderly as you would like. It's important to spend some time on the front end getting it organized so it's easier to work with. Step 4 asks you to take a holistic view of the data—What stands out to you as significant? What is confusing or unexpected? What initial patterns do you see?

The last step (5) is to interpret and report on your analysis informally, through both narrative and graphic representations of your reasoning. Accompanying charts or tables with a written explanation that provides the proper context and study limitations can help lead you and your team to more precise conclusions. To illustrate this, figure 3.5 (page 86) is a sample research brief of quantitative findings related to a hypothetical pilot study on increasing enrollment for female

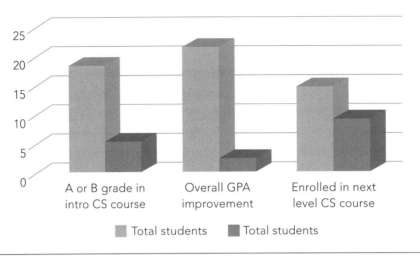

Figure 3.5: Computer science pilot study.

students of color in computer science courses. The goal of this pilot is to increase exposure to computer science, elevate self-esteem and confidence, and spark curiosity for future college and career pathways in STEM professions.

The following is a breakdown of the roles of each pilot study participant, evidence collected, and final interpretation, following Samuels's first five steps of data analysis.

- **Educator role:** All six of the high school's counselors screened nontraditional candidates for participation in an intro to computer science course in the fall. They each identified and met with five tenth-grade female students of color and their parents to share information about the opportunity to enroll in the course.

- **Student role:** Of the thirty students encouraged to enroll, twenty-four added the course to their spring semester schedule. Each student consulted with her counselor four times throughout the semester to check in on progress and receive help if needed. All students took part in online self-paced tutorials outside class as well.

- **Evidence:** Of the twenty-four students enrolled in Introduction to Computer Science, nineteen earned a grade of *B* or higher, while twenty-two of twenty-four improved their overall spring semester grade point average. Fifteen students have enrolled in the next-level computer science course.

- **Interpretation:** With 79 percent of the students earning high grades in the intro course, 91.2 percent increasing their overall GPA—an unforeseen positive impact on their achievement in other classes—and 62.5 percent enrolling in the advanced course, we can conclude that this pilot exceeded our expectations. With such encouraging results, we recommend extending this model to all other high school campuses.

Unless you feel like dusting off some of the tools you learned back in your college statistics class, the next seven steps in Samuel's (2020) procedure could be daunting, as they require technical skills and applications well beyond the basics; therefore, you may decide to outsource these parts to experts or just skip them altogether. Either way, for our purposes, you will obtain adequate information to develop concise theories and inferences from just completing steps 1–5.

QUALITATIVE DATA ANALYSIS

Qualitative data analysis is no less challenging, especially if you immerse yourself in complex coding processes, discourse analysis, or interpretative phenomenological analysis. These are the professional skills and knowledge researchers employ when measuring their subject's characteristics. There are several software programs, such as NVivo, ATLAS.ti, and QDA Miner, which are used to automate qualitative research methods, as well as platforms like Otter.ai that work well for transcribing audio and video recordings. If you have the time and interest and want to make the investment in expertly reviewing focus group notes, case studies, observations, or open-ended survey responses, there are some great resources to get you started.

My best advice is to read and familiarize yourself with qualitative studies related to your topic to see how other scholars approach their work, including Poekert and colleagues' (2020) extensive literature review on leadership for professional learning toward educational equity (as cited in the introduction, page 3). *Research Methods for Social Justice and Equity in Education* is particularly suited to helping novice investigators acquire a sharper understanding of equity-centered research practices as well as pitfalls to avoid and care to take without exacerbating the inequities disenfranchised or marginalized students or families already face on a regular basis (Strunk & Locke, 2019).

FOCUS GROUP FINDINGS

Using the same case study details as in figure 3.5, imagine that the fifteen female tenth graders who decide to enroll in the higher-level course also agreed to take part in a follow-up qualitative investigation. The same five components applied earlier will now be applied to the subsequent scenario, but instead of numerical metrics, subjective criteria are used.

- **Educator role:** The high school's head counselor initiates a focus group to find out more about what motivated the young women to take the next course in the series. She poses four questions to the group, with two neutral observers taking notes.

- **Student role:** The fifteen participants sit in a circle in their high school courtyard with the school counselor and observers and discuss four open-ended prompts for one hour.

- **Evidence:** The assigned documenters record audio and take verbatim notes on what the participants are saying. To maintain the integrity of the conversation, they do not edit students' spoken words. Table 3.2 contains snippets from the group discussion that encapsulate the main motifs and topics the participants bring up in response to the counselor's promptings.

- **Interpretation:** While the group was composed of students from diverse racial and ethnic backgrounds, socioeconomic statuses, and family compositions, they appeared to share a kinship and bond from taking the course together. As each student responded, most of the others indicated frequent affirmation and resonance with her comments with head nods, laughter, and leaning in toward the speaker. The group also seemed to be comfortable enough with the head counselor to answer questions candidly, in their own words, and without signs of apprehension.

Our main conclusions include the following.

- Students feel the need to be invited or encouraged by staff to take coursework that is outside the typical high school schedule or perceived as only for some or certain students.

- Students' self-images dramatically evolved from thoughts and feelings of inadequacy to empowerment by succeeding in the course.

- Embedding multiple and differentiated supports helps students attain new competencies in ways they find comfortable, are attuned to, and can access frequently.

Extrapolating the lessons from this extended hypothetical, leaders may execute variations on the theme in their own environment. While the specifics will be unique, there are overarching data-analysis mixed methodologies you can use to share your findings.

Table 3.2: Focus Group Evidence from Computer Science Pilot

Prompts	Key Themes
Question 1: What were your initial thoughts and feelings about taking your first intro to computer science course?	**Thoughts:** Not good or smart enough; class would be too hard or too much work; didn't really want to drop other fun elective classes; probably going to be the only Puerto Rican girl in there; computer science sounds super boring and nerdy; what will my friends think? **Feelings:** Worried about failing; feeling awkward or lonely; totally anxious about falling behind; kind of excited to try something new; felt special that my counselor thought I could do it; happy that my best friend was taking it too
Question 2: Which of the supports along the way (counselor meetings, tutorials, parent involvement, teacher quality, and so on) most contributed to your success?	**Supports:** Online tutorials were good because I could go at my own pace and repeat lessons; my uncle kept telling me I could do it and family was proud; surprisingly, the teacher was "chill" and funny and seemed like she actually enjoyed teaching us; would have never done this without my counselor pushing and pushing me—did I say pushing . . .?
Question 3: Why did you decide to continue taking computer science next year?	**Reasons:** Guess 'cos I'm a computer science geek now [laughs]; I created a basic program that could be a dope app that'll make me lots of cash if I learn how to do advanced programming; college applications—duh! Seriously, I was getting kind of bored in school, and this is a good challenge
Question 4: What suggestions would you give us (school staff) to increase diversity and representation in other STEM courses?	**Suggestions:** Change the title of the course—it sounds pretty dull, but it's actually not in real life; bring in some people with "cool" careers that can come out of learning these skills; tell the counselors to suggest this course to all students, not just the techies; start younger—I wish I had this in middle school

DATA APPLICATION

This book has provided several case studies in each chapter, which will be summarized in the following table from a data analysis standpoint to accentuate possible applications and nurture meaning-making. You may want to skip back to the scenarios to refresh your memory of the details of the hypotheticals (in the left column) to ground your understanding of the data sources and analysis of the objective in the right column of table 3.3.

Table 3.3: Data Analysis Approaches to Case Study Hypotheticals

Equity-Centered Problem of Practice	Data Source(s) and Analysis Objective(s)
Chapter 1, figure 1.1 (page 20): Policy of involuntary transfer to alternative education placements for credit-deficient seniors who turn eighteen during the spring semester	Evaluate academic transcripts to categorize students by level of credit deficiency to differentiate graduation path options: -15 credits (or 3 failed courses); -20 to 25 credits (4 to 5 failed courses); -30 credits or more (6+ failed courses).
	Correlate home language designations and annual English proficiency assessment scores with students' class schedules to ascertain appropriate course assignments and learning supports.
	Review notes from counseling check-ins with each student to monitor progress on individual credit recovery plan and make realistic adjustments to graduation date targets.
Chapter 2, table 2.1 (page 35): Overidentification of Black males in special education settings based on behaviors	Disaggregate disciplinary referrals or punishments of Black male students by teacher to determine potential trends or patterns that warrant administrative attention.
	Examine implementation fidelity of students' Behavior Intervention Plans prior to placement.
	Review notes from the student study team and IEP meetings to verify appropriateness of placements.

Chapter 2, figure 2.7 (page 48): Chronic absenteeism of socioeconomically disadvantaged K–3 students in rural areas	Break down the district's bus route map and timetables to identify vacuums in service areas to modify potential pick-up and drop-off schedules if necessary.
	Audit schoolwide attendance records to quantify number of absences reportedly due to transportation issues.
	Organize family community meetings at various locations to assess greatest obstacles hindering school attendance.
Chapter 3, figure 3.2 (page 69): Inadequate and unbalanced special education services staffing at district elementary sites due to decentralized hiring protocols	Hold a special principals' meeting to gather ideas related to special education staffing parity across the district and come to consensus on the biggest issues that need resolution.
	Examine recommendations from the school board–convened task force on ways to centralize hiring and placement of special educators at school sites.
	Use the district's current organizational chart to create a data visualization tool (Venn diagram or other graphic representation) to highlight gaps and opportunities for staff assignments and hiring goals.
Chapter 3, case study (page 77): Increase in grade retention requests by third-grade team, disproportionately affecting boys	Gauge parent or caregiver satisfaction with school's retention policy based on anonymous survey responses and parse out areas for staff discussion that reveal higher than 40 percent disagreement.
	Summarize the previous five years' retention referrals in a longitudinal pivot table to assess the degree and source of the problem.
	Conduct a root-cause analysis with first and second grade teachers who also taught the same students being recommended for retention to discover if there were early signs that contributed to later failures.

As demonstrated, data collection and analysis are not a one size fits all endeavor; just as you need to customize supports for different groups of students in order to advance equity, you also must use your professional judgment to pick and choose the most appropriate tools for dissection.

CONCLUSION

Some of you may have felt a little like the young women in the computer science class scenario when reading through and applying the data analysis devices in stage 6—squeamish, tentative, or even a little bit excited. It can be scary to try new things and, on top of that, worry about whether you are correctly interpreting the data or creating conditions that will truly benefit students as a result. But hopefully your passion, drive, and commitment to advancing equity for your students spurred you on. Plus, you have your team. They are an essential checks and balances system to support you in calibrating and validating the findings before settling on any solid conclusions. And they will be with you in the next stage as well before any decree is made to move your initiative forward. Now, on to the stage you've been waiting for: decision-making time!

Feasibility Measures for Educational Pilots

Feasibility Questions	Feasibility Measures
Who is my target population and how can I encourage them to participate?	Requisite number enlisted in the pilot for the duration: Average time from invitation to acceptance, agreement, or commitment:
Are there benefits to randomizing the target population or are preexisting groups sufficient (or preferable)?	Availability of preexisting classes, teams, or departments willing to participate: Proportion of eligible candidates who participate: Proportion of enrolled who stay in the pilot for more than [desired number] sessions, months, meetings, appointments, and so on:
Will I be able to keep participants in the study?	Retention rates for study measures (number that must remain for validity's sake): Anticipated minimum dropout rate acceptable:
Will participants do what they are asked to do?	Adherence rates to study protocols or parameters: Fidelity to which participants implement the initiative as designed:

page 1 of 2

Feasibility Questions	Feasibility Measures
Are the activities or assessments too burdensome?	Proportion of planned assessments that need to be completed: Percentage of activities (such as lessons, trainings, exercises, tasks, or services) executed or performed throughout:
Are the conditions acceptable to participants?	Amount of support or training required: Quantity and quality of necessary materials: Satisfaction ratings (pre-, mid-, and post-trial period):
Are the conditions credible?	Expectation of benefits to targeted groups: Appropriateness of setting or environment: Degree of replicability beyond the pilot:

Source: Adapted from National Center for Complementary and Integrative Health (n.d.). Pilot studies: Common uses and misuses. *Accessed at nccih.nih.gov/grants/pilot-studies-common -uses-and-misuses on December 31, 2022.*

Pilot Planning Template

Directions: Use this planning template with your leadership team to prepare for your equity-centered initiative pilot. Fill out the right column individually or as a team with the goal of coming to consensus.

Critical Questions	Responses
1. What is the scope (and what are the limitations) of the pilot?	The pilot will take place at [locations] for [amount of time]:
	We selected these locations and circumstances for the following equity-related reasons:
2. What do we want to learn through conducting this pilot?	Our equity-centered goals and intentions behind this pilot are:
	We hope to discover:
3. How will we know if we've learned what we need from the pilot?	We will use the following formative tools to collect data on the intended student groups' progress:
	We will analyze and interpret the data using these methods:
4. What will we do to intervene when or if it's not going well?	We will look for these indicators that interventions or adaptations may be needed to better support underserved students' learning goals:
	Our intervention plan will include these possible strategies:

Critical Questions	Responses
5. What will we do to expand on early successes?	We will look for these indicators that we are exceeding our original goals:
	Our expansion plans will include these possible strategies:
6. How will we determine whether to terminate, continue, or expand the pilot?	After running the pilot for [period of time] and collecting [feedback, data, and observations], we will meet on [date] to determine next steps.
	Our decision making will include the following equity-based thresholds or metrics:

Additional considerations:

Continuum of Stakeholder Groups

Part I Directions: In the following spaces, list the groups who have the most and least interest and influence related to the equity-centered initiative.

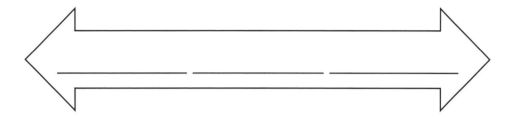

Part II: Write down the outreach mechanisms you will employ for engagement with the three categories of stakeholders.

Outreach Strategies for Obstructers:

Outreach Strategies for Observers:

Outreach Strategies for Organizers:

Engagement Strategies

Directions: The left column contains each of Maslow's (1943, 1954) categories along with a key tenet describing the need. The middle column offers suggestions for leadership teams to contemplate and plan for outreach with a focus on equity. The right column is designed for leadership teams to add specific details for their own locales regarding each level on the hierarchy.

Maslow's Hierarchy of Needs	Guiding Questions for Equity-Centered Family and Community Engagement	Team Planning Notes for Engagement Sessions
Level 5: Self-Actualization Tenet: Achieving Potential or Mastery	What is the purpose of the outreach? How can we deliver on participants' expectations? What kinds of active roles can we give participants? How might we personalize the experience? What kinds of expertise or professional experience can be tapped from people in the room? What is the problem we are trying to solve? How can we utilize collective knowledge and skill sets? What types of high-level critical thinking tasks should we employ?	
Level 4: Self-Esteem Tenet: Acceptance	How can we honor all cultures, languages, and background experiences in the room? What are some mechanisms we might use to validate suggestions? How should we differentiate instruction for a range of participants? How might we offer appreciation or encouragement to open discussion? How will we let people know that we respect their involvement by setting and committing to norms? When and how will we check for understanding using the audience's native languages?	

Maslow's Hierarchy of Needs	Guiding Questions for Equity-Centered Family and Community Engagement	Team Planning Notes for Engagement Sessions
Level 3: Love and Belonging Tenet: Relationships	Who will we ask to make personalized invitations or phone calls? Who will coordinate the volunteers to guide people from the parking lot to the meeting space? Who will design and post multilingual welcome and directional signs and greet participants at the door? How might we arrange tables and chairs to boost interactions? What kinds of nonthreatening icebreakers might help build a feeling of community? How might the facilitator use an anecdote or personal story to set the tone? What different cultures are in the room and how might those participants best respond to engaging in group activities? How can we encourage work in collaborative teams?	
Level 2: Safety Tenet: Comfort	Who will be responsible for monitoring the heat or air conditioning to moderate temperatures? What are the most convenient and centralized locations for maximum participation? How will we ensure accessibility for people with disabilities? How will we address unintentional stereotyping or bias from others? What are some other kinds of comforts we can provide?	

page 2 of 3

Maslow's Hierarchy of Needs	Guiding Questions for Equity-Centered Family and Community Engagement	Team Planning Notes for Engagement Sessions
Level 1: Physiological Well-Being Tenet: Food, Shelter, Health	Who will coordinate and provide on-site childcare during the meeting? What kinds of snacks or meals should we have available that are considerate of religious and cultural principles (such as vegetarianism, veganism, Kosher, Halal, and so on)? How can we extend transportation options (for example, transit maps, tickets, free parking)? What kinds of arrangements do we need to make for inclement weather? What are some places we can leverage that are meaningful to the community (for example, community center, apartment complex courtyard, religious institutions)? How will we stagger meeting times to accommodate caregivers' various work and home schedules? Are there any appropriate takeaways or door prizes we can offer?	

Source: Maslow, A. H. (1943). A theory of human motivation. Psychological Review, 50*(4), 370–396;* Maslow, A. H. (1954). Motivation and personality. *New York: Harper & Row.*

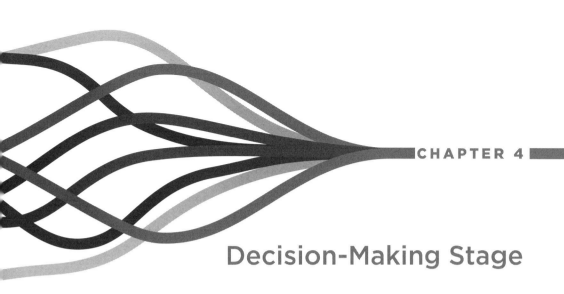

CHAPTER 4

Decision-Making Stage

Decision making is both an art and a science. You've done a lot of the science part already during the three trial stages described in the previous chapter—commencing multiple experiments, harvesting rich information, and interpreting it to the best of your ability—all with the goal of ele-

> ### KEY CONCEPTS
>
> **Stage 7: Decide.** Make a final choice on whether to implement your initiative.

vating previously underserved students' learning experiences in your school and district. The art of decision making is not so clinical, simply because there can never be enough inputs in the universe to safeguard against every risk or guarantee complete success.

Many of the conventional words of wisdom on the topic pertain to psychology-based decision making—as in choosing a personal course of action out of several available options: Should I buy this house or that condo? Should I join a gym, work out at home, or take a yoga class? Should I approach my boss about my work schedule or just live with it? and so on. But what about when you are tasked with making critical decisions on behalf of an organization? As a leader, that's a major part of your job, so don't be afraid of the *what ifs* that would otherwise prevent you from making a decision. While it's impossible to get it 100 percent right, you will have many more opportunities to use continuous improvement practices to amend the implementation as real-life circumstances unfold.

Up to this point, this book has clustered the stages into trios and will return to that model after this chapter. This chapter departs from that format to address stage 7, *Decide*, as its own entity. The reason it's separated is to draw a bright line between preparation and implementation. It's the demarcation point at which the ten-stage process ends and you move on to other projects or you fully commit to setting the initiative in motion. In *Leading the Launch*, I used traffic control signal imagery to illustrate the three options you have in front of you: (1) red means *stop*, (2) yellow means *slow down*, and (3) green means *go* (Wallace, 2022). It's a simple and universal concept that most people around the globe can relate to.

Leading the Launch includes a reproducible decision-making rubric and assessment to help teams come to a collective decision on green-lighting, yellow-lighting, or red-lighting the initiative (Wallace, 2022). For the sake of expediency, I don't go further into the red or yellow light situations other than to say that red is done. Let it go. Yellow is on hold until the situation changes. So our focus is squarely on *how* to navigate the actual approval channels in your school or district that go beyond the team's recommendation to green-light an implementation.

That process doesn't change significantly in this version, except to ask your team to center equity more overtly, as shown in figure 4.1. Each team member is asked to evaluate the initiative against the work conducted in stages 1–6 of the implementation process before coming to agreement on an endorsement.

Stage 1–6 Criteria	Red	Yellow	Green
1. Research and planning was conducted with a clear equity focus.	Insufficient	Sufficient	Excellent
2. Proposal demonstrated a deep understanding of the equity-centered problem of practice.	Weak	Adequate	Strong
3. Prioritization process revealed urgency to rank the initiative and schedule its debut.	Low	Medium	High
4. Pilot showed sufficient progress or achievement within identified student groups.	Unsatisfactory	Satisfactory	Successful
5. The feedback and input by key stakeholders during engagement outreach was encouraging.	Negative	Mixed	Positive
6. Data analysis makes a compelling case to launch the initiative full scale.	Unclear	Inconclusive or mixed	Compelling

Figure 4.1: Initiative evaluation.

*Visit **go.SolutionTree.com/diversityandequity** for a free reproducible version of this figure.*

STAGE 7: DECIDE

While not explicitly stated yet, the ten-stage process as related to equity-centered initiatives is one that imbues mind, body, and spirit. Education is about people. And what makes us human is our capacity to integrate our feelings and thoughts into action. Yinying Wang (2019) advises us to balance data-driven with moral or heart-led decision making. If we compartmentalize too much in the analytical realm, we might miss some valuable instincts and gut feelings. If feelings go unchecked, however, without tapping into our logical or objective ethos, our judgments might be made impulsively or with blinders on. As such, don't become too enamored with your clinical data at the risk of sacrificing the impact on humanity. At the same time, don't say *yes* to an initiative just because it feels good but has little substance to back it up. This is why a team approach has been reiterated throughout the new initiative protocol. If you've selected a diverse sounding board—the thinkers and feelers, sensors and intuitivists, introverts and extroverts, perceivers and judgers, and everyone in-between (for more on these personality traits, check out this article on Myers-Briggs teacher personality types by Stephen Rushton, Jackson Morgan, and Michael Richard [2007])—you will bring harmony and symmetry to stage 7 (Cristofaro, 2017).

THE APPROVAL PROCESS

Once the decision to green-light is agreed on, leaders must learn (if they do not already know) how to obtain formal authorization. Each district or county office has its own procedures, governance, and policies for approving new programs. While the nuances are surely unique to each, most educational organizations include some combination of these compliance mechanisms: budget or fiscal, departmental or committee, governance board, or bargaining unit vote (if all or part of the implementation is negotiable per the employee association–district collective bargaining agreement). Figure 4.2 (page 104) depicts a generic diagram of how an approval process might flow.

Jumping through the hoops of decision making can be tricky but readily accomplished if you know how to work the system. Districts and counties are bureaucratic institutions that function via a series of checks and balances. You must *pass go* at every level or face getting kicked back a step or two, which will delay your implementation. It's advantageous to map backward from the school board meeting approval date, especially since many of the preliminary steps are prescheduled by meeting or regular review dates.

Pioneers of backward instructional planning Grant Wiggins and Jay McTighe's seminal work *Understanding by Design* (2005) has influenced generations of

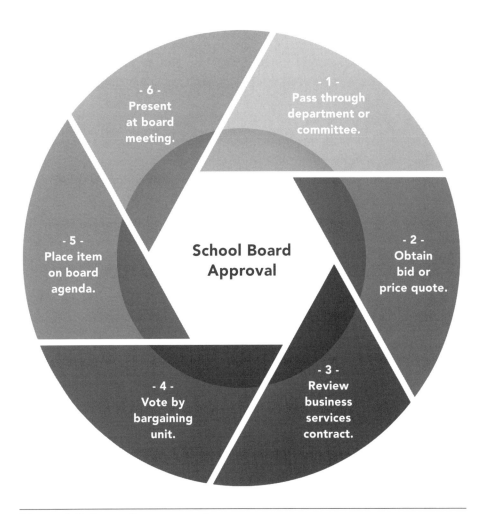

Figure 4.2: Steps for approval.

educators' methods of lesson and unit planning. The underlying rationale is that a teacher starts with the end goal or learning objective they want students to achieve and then intentionally plans backward each of the prior steps that will best help them reach those intended accomplishments. While this design model is primarily geared toward classroom teachers, it can also be converted to leadership practices.

The three stages Wiggins and McTighe (2005) outline include "1) Identify desired results; 2) Determine acceptable evidence, and 3) Plan learning experiences and instruction" (p. 18). This might be translated in these ways to an administrator's scope of work: (1) identify desired equity-centered goals or outcomes; (2) determine appropriate measures that indicate advantageous impacts on designated student populations, and (3) acquire materials and resources and establish processes to set the stage for implementation. The scenario that follows shows how this revised framework can be leveraged to promote social justice for student groups.

SCENARIO

While many examples in this book have been affiliated with instructional initiatives, we'll switch gears now to an example of how infrastructure upgrades also play a key role in advancing equity. Mary Filardo, Jeffrey M. Vincent, and Kevin Sullivan (2018) cite several research studies and court cases that correlate student achievement with high-quality facilities. They state, "Not only are school facilities important to student and teacher health and performance, they are vital community assets. Public school facilities, often as the centers of their communities, act as 'equity hubs' for numerous social service programs" (Filardo et al., 2018, p. 4). Maintenance and facilities initiatives can be complicated as the components for erecting an entire building are likely not as familiar to an educational leader as curriculum-based launches are. But we can't only focus on teaching and learning when the environment needs attention as well. Campus beautification and upkeep can go a long way toward making staff, students, and families feel nurtured and valued, especially in high-needs, low-resourced communities.

Figure 4.3 delineates a plan a high school building principal must work through to seek approval to construct a state-of-the-art theater at the district's only (and lowest-achieving) secondary school without a performing arts space.

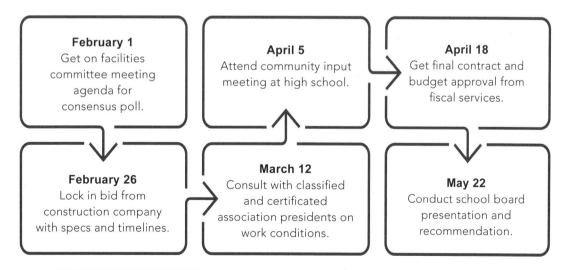

February 1
Get on facilities committee meeting agenda for consensus poll.

April 5
Attend community input meeting at high school.

April 18
Get final contract and budget approval from fiscal services.

February 26
Lock in bid from construction company with specs and timelines.

March 12
Consult with classified and certificated association presidents on work conditions.

May 22
Conduct school board presentation and recommendation.

Figure 4.3: Timeline and path to performance arts theater approval.

To get the construction timeline on pace for opening the theater before the fall musical, the principal needs to hit several benchmarks before breaking ground.

But prior to calendaring the vital checkpoints, she uses the adapted *Understanding by Design* (Wiggins & McTighe, 2005) stages for school leaders to organize her project. These prompts, plus a calendar mapping tool adapted from figure 4.3 (page 105), are included in the reproducibles section at the end of this chapter (page 114).

1. Identify desired equity-centered goals or outcomes.

    a. Institute elective offerings that build skills (stage design, construction, and work experience), career competencies (public speaking, collaboration, and responsibility), and personal fulfillment (music, acting, and play), with priority enrollment for students of color and from low socioeconomic backgrounds.

    b. Provide creative outlets and means of self-expression for marginalized student groups to impart and magnify their own cultures and ancestry on stage.

    c. Infuse the school climate with lively energy and collective pride that celebrates diversity and unifies majority and minority groups in a shared space.

    d. Enrich learning experiences and exposure to the arts for those who might not have access to it otherwise.

2. Determine appropriate measures that indicate advantageous impacts on designated student populations.

    a. The school becomes a desirable destination for transfer students, and enrollment growth results in expansion of elective course offerings for current students.

    b. Achievement of facilities parity with other schools with performing arts complexes boosts participation in school and community gatherings.

    c. Increase attendance and decrease disciplinary consequences for students enrolled in drama, music, clubs, or other performance activities.

3. Acquire materials and resources and establish processes to set the stage for implementation.

    a. Map out proposed locations on campus and examine the pros and cons of each option.

b. Engage the surrounding community to generate support for a neighborhood theater.

c. Develop and present compelling arguments to gain school board approval.

d. Request a meeting with the business services department to find out cost estimates and instructions on how to proceed with a construction bidding process.

e. Investigate potential funding sources and fundraisers to offset some of the costs.

f. Adopt a project management tool to monitor progress and keep the schedule on track.

After meeting each goal, the principal is able to get the theater ready for opening night and celebrates by hosting a communitywide event, dedicating the building to a local Latina playwright who got her start at the school.

SCHOOL BOARD ENGAGEMENT

Now for a few words on the roles, functions, and parameters of governance teams. If leaders don't already know what model governs their own system, it's a high priority to learn. Many districts in the United States and Canada have three-, five-, seven-, or nine-member elected school boards or education councils. According to the National School Boards Association survey (2018), there are "90,000 school board members, mostly [locally] elected (88% v. 12% [appointed]), who govern the [United States'] 13,500 school districts" (p. 2). Other less common models include tribal or communal, staff self-governed, or mayoral-run school districts. Since the vast majority operate with an elected board, that will be our focus in this section.

Janice Jackson and Monette McIver (n.d.) note that in the United States:

> Board members/trustees set and monitor policy implementation as well as approve the allocation of resources across the system. Along with the superintendent/charter CEO, whom they are responsible for hiring, they set the vision and mission for the organization. A key aspect of that vision is the commitment to be an organization in which equity is core to the quality of the work.

More often than not, school boards are overwhelmingly composed of elected non-educator members whose minimum criteria to hold office include being (1) eighteen years or older and (2) a resident of the neighborhood, city, or county.

They may be local businesspeople, parents of students in the district, community activists, or budding politicians. Bear this in mind when deciding what information to share, how to share it, and in what modes. Your aim is clarity. Keep language free of jargon and acronyms and make the call to action obvious so they know what they are voting on.

Since sanctioning by some sort of governing body is typically the final step of an approval process, it's critical to make sure the board of trustees or directors have been sufficiently informed starting as early as stage 3, but most certainly throughout stages 4–6. Boards don't like surprises. Boards don't relish lines of people wrapped around the building waiting to complain about your initiative at public comment. Boards want to feel secure that they have all they need to know before voting. Some boards like hard facts, some like stories, some like having the big picture, and some like nitty-gritty details—but all love to hear from happy students and parents. Consider what you need to include to get your particular governance team to *yes*. The tools included in this section are effective for prepping your governing members.

Many superintendents find that sending a weekly update or memo to the school board is an excellent way to keep members apprised of new developments in the district. Because school board members are often recognizable figures in their community, they also must be ready to respond to hot topics should members of the public bring them up when they run into each other at the grocery store or at a restaurant on the weekend. Weekly updates contain short blurbs submitted by the assistant superintendents or directors from the business services, instructional services, and human resources departments for inclusion whenever significant. Figure 4.4 is a model memo.

There are several clues in figure 4.4 that point out the following deliberate elements to think about embedding in your own version.

- Briefly orient the board to past and current circumstances on the topic.

- Remind the board of equity-centered goals they had a hand in developing.

- Share one or two pieces of compelling data to establish urgency to address the existing inequities.

- Provide dates and events where the board was previously informed of the pilot initiation.

- Let them know when they can expect you to check back in.

MEMO

To: District Board of Trustees   **From:** Superintendent

Topic: Attendance Program Pilot Update

As you well know, some of the major goals for this current school year have been to ensure that our students are safe, cared for, and ready to learn. Prior to this school year, our district has historically had a 94 percent average daily attendance rate. The data we collected from the last half of the academic year shows that rate has decreased to 86 percent. This highly impacts our district's fiscal solvency, and we stand to lose $4.7 million a year as a result.

However, even more important than the financial consequences, the data reveals that of the 8 percent chronically truant students, over half are designated as students in foster homes and students experiencing homelessness. You may remember the discussion at our board retreat this fall, about staff's intention to launch a pilot for an online attendance and truancy prevention program to systematize our attendance monitoring. As an equity-centered school district, our charge is to intervene swiftly with ample strategies to keep our students most at risk from falling through the cracks.

Over the first three months of the year, we have been able to identify 119 students who needed intervention measures to improve their attendance, as well as more aggressive approaches to support the 8 percent of students who have been identified as critically at risk of chronic truancy and dropping out. We have been able to contact each and every caregiver in the district with a list of community resources, daily motivational social media posts, and on-the-spot attendance data; as a result, we've already witnessed an encouraging increase to 89 percent average daily student attendance from September through November, with 2 percent of the 3 percent gain a direct result of our concentrated attention on our students in foster and homeless situations.

The attached document contains two reports from the online platform that create guidepost opportunities for improvement and will spur us to continue to set increased goals for second part of the pilot. At the conclusion of the pilot and stakeholder engagement sessions, I will send you another progress report prior to receiving the leadership team's recommendation at a future board meeting. In the meantime, if you'd like a personal view of how the product works, I will arrange for staff to demonstrate it for you an hour before next week's board meeting.

In closing, I'll leave you with this quote from a student who has recently resumed attending school regularly: He said, "I thought you didn't care. That I didn't matter. But now I see that you're not going to leave me alone, so I might as well come to school so you can just bug me in person." Here's to bugging more students into getting back to school going forward!

Figure 4.4: Memo to school board regarding attendance pilot.

- Invite them to observe the pilot, at an appropriate time.

- Present any initial findings that the pilot is forecasting promising results.

- Reference places to find more detailed data or learn more about the program.

- Leave them with a final thought that humanizes the effect of the initiative on the actual people it is meant to impact.

- Spell out acronyms the first time they are used and define any education-related terms that the public might not understand.

- Keep it under two pages—anything else should be included as an attachment or link.

Using a variation of figure 4.4 (page 109), customize the template in figure 4.5 to report progress on a current pilot or implementation. (See page 115 for a blank reproducible of this figure.)

The front-loading you do up to stage 7 can only help you predict where the board's concerns are early on, plus create a foundation for the governing body to refer to when it sees the item on the agenda, such as in the following examples. Figure 4.6 (page 112) and figure 4.7 (page 113) mimic the model in figure 4.4. (See page 117 for a blank reproducible version of figure 4.7).

Figure 4.2 (page 104) suggested the typical steps it takes to get to board approval, but the work doesn't end there. Once authorized, your team will need to complete the bureaucratic processes that, depending on the nature of the initiative, may include submitting purchase orders, hiring or training for new positions, scheduling materials deliveries to school sites, and coordinating logistics for the rollout. Some of this foundation can be laid concurrently with the approval process as long as you stay within your organization's established bounds of protocol.

CONCLUSION

Feels good, doesn't it? This is probably way more time and energy than you've ever spent launching a new initiative "the old way." That familiar adage *go slow to go fast* certainly applies here. All the prior stages' tasks have been checked off the list. It's almost launch time. The next chapter will cover the final three execution stages in the process that will determine the lasting success and impact of your equity-centered initiative!

MEMO

To: [Governing body name]   **From:** Superintendent [name]

Date: [Month, day, year]   **Topic:** [Pilot name] Pilot Update

[Historical or current situation]

As you are aware, our goals this school year have been to ensure that our district's students receive equitable access to [academic, extracurricular program, facilities, or courses]. While we have faced many challenges as a district meeting [student group]'s needs, we are continuing to learn, grow, and find solutions to [improve achievement, advance equitable conditions, or repair harm].

Our district has historically [add relevant data points]. The information we've collected from the [time period] shows that we are on track for [improvement or decline] in our current environment.

[Pilot status]

Per your earlier consent, since [month day, year] we have partnered with [solution provider, company, or organization] to [add service or product], allowing us to intervene swiftly with ample strategies to keep our students from falling through the cracks. Over the course of the first [number of months] months of the year, we have been able to identify [number of students] students that needed [add details], as well as more strident approaches to support the [percent] percent of students who are even more critically at risk.

[Initial findings]

[Strategy or program] has assisted us in providing these resources [add details] for [number of] students. As a result we've witnessed [quantifiable or qualitative] impact on [student group]'s progress between [date started and current date]. These initial findings are promising indeed!

[Forecasting]

While we don't yet know what the ultimate outcomes of this pilot will be, we do know that having multiple data points to guide our actions is essential. The attached document contains [number of] reports that create opportunities for improvement and will help us continue to set goals for the upcoming school year. You can also click on this [link] that will bring you to a [product website or district database] with more detailed information. Please let me know what questions you may have or if you would like to visit the pilot site at [location] to see how it's rolling out.

[Personal or uplifting anecdote or observation]

In closing, I'll leave you with this **[humanizing message].**

Figure 4.5: School board memo template.

Title: Adoption of Attendance Accounting and Reporting Platform

Category: Regular agenda item

Type: Presentation approval   **Date:** June 2022

Recommended action: Approve automated student attendance tracking, prevention, and intervention program for the upcoming school year.

Background:
Due to the COVID-19 pandemic, every student in our district was placed in a remote learning environment for the remainder of the 2019–2020 school year. In compliance with local and state orders, we provided online instruction for all K–12 students through the summer of 2020, while gathering feedback and developing several options for the opening of the next academic year. Based on stakeholder input, health orders, employee unit negotiations, and guidance from the county office of education, our district elected to provide instruction in hybrid and fully virtual modes in fall 2020. At the semester, we ceased fully online teaching and shifted to an option of hybrid or in-person model starting in January 2021.

Current status:
While it has been our regular practice to carefully monitor student attendance annually, the current school year has prompted staff to increase efforts to keep students engaged and actively attending, especially in hybrid classrooms. Studies have shown that our most underserved and vulnerable families now need more support than ever to achieve equity and close performance gaps post-pandemic. In our own district's case, those groups include students in foster care or experiencing homelessness; families with low socioeconomic status, especially in rural areas; and students with disabilities or special education students.

The attendance tracking system we piloted this fall has been extremely illuminating in supplying us with tools, information, strategies, and cutting-edge technologies to identify students with concerning attendance patterns in order to get them back on track with their education. This presentation will include data and reports from our student information system and the truancy and dropout prevention program, both of which show the early impacts from interventions used with students struggling academically, social-emotionally, or in their home environments during these challenging times.

The program incorporated several levels of intervention, which are included in the attachment titled *Annual Attendance Report*. In that document, demographic breakdowns and disaggregated data are also provided as evidence of the program's preliminary successes. In short, we have been able to discover that 3 to 4 percent of our previously chronically absentee students in foster or homeless situations have resumed regular schooling since starting the pilot, and all other student groups have trended upward as well. We are currently only two percentage points away from returning to our pre-pandemic attendance rate of 94 percent.

Recommendation:
The director of student services recommends that the board of trustees approves a three-year agreement for a truancy and dropout prevention system. In addition, staff requests additional direction from the board to develop long-term attendance incentives in our district.

Board or district goals:
This program will help the district meet the following goals or actions in our local accountability plan:

- Improve attendance for all students with less than 85 percent regular attendance, with a focus on students in foster care or experiencing homelessness, students with disabilities or special education students, and students from low socioeconomic areas within our boundaries.

- Increase outreach to families by providing resources, support, and strategies for school readiness.

Policy Implications:
This presentation is consistent with Board Policy 1111.1 and Education Code 2222.2.

Attachments:
Slide deck; *Annual Attendance Report*; contract with truancy and dropout prevention system

Figure 4.6: Request for school board approval of attendance program.

Title: Adoption of [program, product, or process system]

Category: [Regular consent] agenda item

Type: [Presentation approval]   **Date:** [Month, day, year]

Recommended Action: Approve [program, product, or system]

Background:
[Add recent history leading up to the pilot or trial period related to the initiative]
[Add rationale or district goals]
[Add student groups the initiative is focused on]

Current status:
[Provide information related to results from pilot]
[Briefly explain initial findings]
[Include one or two data points that illustrate progress]
[Refer to any attached supporting documents or links]

Recommendation:
[Add the presenter or leader's name and title]
[Spell out the exact recommendation]
[Suggest any future direction requested]

Board or district goals:
[List the equity-centered goals or actions this program or product will help meet]

Policy implications:
[Reference board policy, state education code, or other guidance documents]

Attachments:

Figure 4.7: School board agenda item template.

Backward Planning Template and Timeline

1. Identify desired equity-centered goals or outcomes:

    a.

    b.

    c.

2. Determine appropriate measures that indicate advantageous impacts on designated student populations:

    a.

    b.

    c.

3. Acquire materials and resources and establish processes to set the stage for implementation:

    a.

    b.

    c.

Process Timeline: Provide the date and a brief description of the benchmark that needs to be met in order to stay on track with project deadlines.

School Board Memo Template

To: [Governing body name]

From: Superintendent [name]

Date: [Month, day, year]

Topic: [Pilot name] Pilot Update

[Historical or current situation]
As you are aware, our goals this school year have been to ensure that our district's students receive equitable access to **[academic, extracurricular program, facilities, or courses]**. While we have faced many challenges as a district meeting **[student group]**'s needs, we are continuing to learn, grow, and find solutions to **[improve achievement, advance equitable conditions, or repair harm]**.

Our district has historically **[add relevant data points]**. The information we've collected from the [time period] shows that we are on track for **[improvement or decline]** in our current environment.

[Pilot status]

Per your earlier consent, since **[month, day, year]** we have partnered with **[solution provider, company, or organization]** to **[add service or product]**, allowing us to intervene swiftly with ample strategies to keep our students from falling through the cracks. Over the course of the first **[number of months]** months of the year, we have been able to identify **[number of students]** students that needed **[add details]**, as well as more strident approaches to support the **[percent]** percent of students who are even more critically at risk.

page 1 of 2

[Initial findings]

[Strategy or program] has assisted us in providing these resources **[add details]** for **[number of]** students. As a result we've witnessed **[quantifiable or qualitative]** impact on **[student group]**'s progress between **[date started and current date]**. These initial findings are promising indeed!

[Forecasting]

While we don't yet know what the ultimate outcomes of this pilot will be, we do know that having multiple data points to guide our actions is essential. The attached document contains **[number of]** reports that create opportunities for improvement and will help us continue to set goals for the upcoming school year. You can also click on this **[link]** that will bring you to a **[product website or district database]** with more detailed information. Please let me know what questions you may have or if you would like to visit the pilot site at **[location]** to see how it's rolling out.

[Personal or uplifting anecdote or observation]

In closing, I'll leave you with this **[humanizing message]**.

School Board Agenda Item Template

Title:

Category:

Type:

Date:

Recommended Action:

Background:
(Add recent history leading up to the pilot or trial period related to the initiative, rationale or district goals, and student groups the initiative is focused on.)

Current status:
(Provide information related to results from pilot and briefly explain initial findings. Include one or two data points that illustrate progress. Refer to any attached supporting documents or links.)

Recommendation:
(Add the presenter or leader's name and title, spell out the exact recommendation, and suggest any future direction requested.)

Board or district goals:
(List the equity-centered goals or actions this program or product will help meet.)

Policy implications:
(Reference board policy, state education code, or other guidance documents.)

Attachments:

CHAPTER 5

Execution Stages

Isn't it gratifying to have had your equity-centered initiative blessed by the powers that be and begin to take shape as an adopted program, policy, or process in the organization? *That's big.* Navigating the first seven stages has made you the go-to local expert on the problem of practice, but also a trailblazer for those whom you will inspire to do the same. Our industry needs role models like you to encourage others to take up the mantle of their own special missions on behalf of the historically underserved

KEY CONCEPTS

Stage 8: Teach. Train peers in skills and knowledge they need to participate in your initiative.

Stage 9: Launch. Officially implement your initiative.

Stage 10: Sustain. Ensure longevity and enthusiasm for your initiative.

in our schools. Not only are you changing students' lives but also reinvigorating what originally called you and your peers to the field of educational leadership. We don't hear the words *thank you* as much as we should, so let me sincerely do so here. Thank you. Your extraordinary efforts are making a major difference.

The final three stages shift the leadership team's eyes to execution. First, you need to assess and determine staff's learning needs in stage 8 (Teach). What skills, knowledge, and mindsets are critical to attain and possess for the initiative to land as intended? If it's highly technical or requires significant changes to how things have been historically done, you'll need to spend an ample amount of time in professional learning and training activities. But the instruction doesn't end there; throughout the launch period itself in stage 9 (Launch) and thereafter in stage 10 (Sustain), leaders will also need to plan for and deliver ongoing high-quality job-embedded coaching, guidance, and practice opportunities. This chapter is best introduced via this first sentence in Andy Hargreaves and Dean Fink's (2006) book *Sustainable Leadership*: "Change in education is easy to propose, hard to implement, and extraordinarily difficult to sustain" (p. 1). The good news is, the activities and prompts in this chapter will secure those latter two dynamics so you finish strong.

STAGE 8: TEACH

The teaching part should be simple, right? After all, that's why we all went into education in the first place. In truth, teaching adults is actually not simple at all. We've all been in that participant seat, and we've all seen the memes and cartoons lamenting in-service days, icebreakers, and shared stories from past (cringeworthy) professional development sessions. Reflect for a moment on the worst and best training experiences you've had during your career. Your goal is to replicate the best and avoid elements of the worst so your hard work in stages 1–7 is not unraveled in a single day.

There have been volumes written on best practices in professional learning that you can use as a foundation if you are new to the arena. I'd recommend jumping onto the Learning Policy Institute (https://learningpolicyinstitute.org), Learning Forward (https://learningforward.org), and ASCD (https://acsd.org/learning) websites to browse their articles, blogs, videos, and check out their webinars and conferences. Our focus in this section is to explore a bit further how equity-centered professional learning can be executed in ways that respect adults and the student groups they are impacting. Director of external research for EL education, Meg Riordan, professor at Montclair State University, Emily J. Klein, and graduate student in the teacher education program at Montclair State University, Catherine Gaynor, (2019) contend the following:

> As we understand student learning to be grounded in the needs of students, teachers also must have the opportunity to experience professional learning that honors their needs in a meaningful way (Skerrett, Warrington, & Williamson, 2018). Skerrett et al. (2018) identified six features to support the professional development as equity educators: teacher identified and driven, presented by experts who value the teachers' expertise, context where the teachers can be the teacher and the learner, sustained over time with continued further learning, fosters meaningful collaborative relationships with others in the community, and includes support from those with the capital to enact change. Providing professional development with these

features allows teachers to experience more equitable educational practices in their own learning. (p. 330)

Equity is a two-way street. When we design and model professional learning for staff that considers their professional experiences, attends to their personal needs, and values their time and involvement, it catalyzes how they implement the initiative in their work setting. Dorinda J. Carter Andrews and Gail Richmond (2019) further emphasize this point for reframing our view of effective professional learning:

> We assert the need for an expanded view of what is meant by "effective PD" as inclusive of equity as not only essential for student learners but also for teacher learners. . . . Teachers, whose professional identity includes an asset-based pedagogical orientation toward learning, draw on the cultural strengths and native learning modalities of students. When teachers are able to build their collective efficacy around shared goals related to sustaining students' cultural assets and building on students' strengths, these shared beliefs can significantly positively influence student learning. (p. 408)

Putting this research into practice does not happen by accident. *Leading the Launch* supplies practitioners a planning worksheet to intentionally design professional learning experiences with the staff needs at the center (Wallace, 2022). It includes the content focus, active learning and participation opportunities, periodic formative assessments, job-embedded collaboration, modeling, coaching and support, feedback and reflection, and sustained duration. Since the first version is a more generalized tool that can apply to any initiative, the following version includes a supplemental section meant to keep equity as the focus (see figure 5.1, page 122). (See page 146 for a blank reproducible version of this supplemental section.)

These additional prompts lead us to the next section on what motivates adult learners and the competencies they bring to the table.

MOTIVATIONS AND COMPETENCIES

Think about the things that motivate you as a leader and how those on your own staff also possess a range of inclinations and dispositions. Some respond well to praise and recognition while others may act out of fear of failure or avoidance of punishment; some may be driven by financial compensation or other extrinsic rewards, and others by the enjoyment of feeling intrinsically fulfilled by a

Directions: This worksheet is intended to ensure a well-rounded educational experience for your teachers and staff. Complete each prompt with your team for planning your professional development.

Prompts for Key Features of Design: Team Response
Equity Lens Describe how the specific equity problem of practice will be introduced and referenced throughout the staff learning experiences: How we will leverage our own students' voices, experiences, and data to personalize the training and establish urgency: How we will respond to deficit language, push-back, or refusal to acknowledge inequities exist in our system:

Content Focused
 	
1. Content or concepts to deliver:
 	
2. The learning objectives are:
 	
3. The majority of participants are likely to:
    a. Be familiar with the topic or content
    b. Be somewhat knowledgeable
    c. Not have any experience with it
4. On a scale of 1–5, the concepts are easy (1) or difficult (5) to grasp: 1 2 3 4 5

Active Learning 1. We will actively engage participants at a minimum of every fifteen to twenty minutes by: 2. The three different interactive methods we will use to involve the audience in higher-level learning activities are: 3. The formative assessments we will use to check for understanding are:

Job-Embedded Collaboration

1. We will connect the participants' learning in the session to their daily work by:

2. What participants learn in the session will be reinforced on the job in the following ways:

3. We will ensure that participants will have opportunities to collaborate in between trainings by:

Models

We will employ the following demonstrations, case studies, or scenarios to illustrate key learning objectives.

1. Our exemplars have been screened in the following ways to ensure that they are free from bias, stereotypes, and discrimination of students, families, or employee groups:

2. We will invite participants to connect their own real-life work situations with the demonstrated models by:

Coaching and Support

1. We will provide instructional coaches or other expert support:
   a. Prior to the professional development session
   b. During the professional development session
   c. After the professional development session

2. Our coaches and experts will be available to help participants by:

3. Technical support will be provided by the _____ departments in the following ways:

Figure 5.1: Professional development design worksheet. continued ▶

Prompts for Key Features of Design: Team Response

Feedback and Reflection

1. At the beginning of the session, we will ask participants to share with us:

2. At a mid-point in the session, we will ask for feedback on:

3. After the session, we will use the following tool to reflect on strengths and weaknesses and plan next steps:

Sustained Duration

1. This professional development is most appropriately delivered:

    a. In a single session for a heterogeneous audience

    b. In several sessions for a heterogeneous audience

    c. In a single session differentiated by skill/knowledge/specialized groups

    d. In several sessions differentiated by skill/knowledge/specialized groups

    e. Other:

2. How long will it generally take for most participants to gain mastery over the subject or content?

3. We will revisit and reinforce the content throughout the school year through these means:

Source: Adapted from Wallace, 2022.

compelling project. What personally motivates people differs from individual to individual, but there are a few human tendencies we have in common.

In the workplace, Richard M. Ryan and Edward L. Deci's (2000) self-determination theory postulates that we share "*three innate psychological needs—competence, autonomy, and relatedness—which when satisfied yield enhanced self-motivation and mental health and when thwarted lead to diminished motivation and well-being*" (p. 68). Let's unpack these further.

- *Competence* is the belief that one can achieve their objectivation or goals and possess ample support, knowledge, and skills to do so.

- *Autonomy* is about locus of control; when offered self-determination, people feel trusted and expected to make good decisions and contribute in their own unique ways to the organization, without rebuke.

- *Relatedness* means that we can see ourselves as an essential player on a team that we care for, and on which we have a meaningful role to help reach a mutually shared purpose.

Keeping these forces in mind, we'll take the planning document one leap forward and return to the iceberg metaphor from chapter 1 (page 20). Instead of organizational culture, let's explore how the human iceberg operates and can be leveraged for creating the conditions for transformative learning events. Siti Noor Ismail, Shamsuddin Muhammad, Mohd Norakmar Omar, and Arumugam Raman (2020) note that "ongoing training . . . is a vital element in developing an individual's potential for coping with future challenges" (p. 2438) and reference the model in figure 5.2 (page 126) to examine how instructional leadership can influence teachers' 21st century functional competencies.

As with all iceberg models, the top part represents the limited percentage of what we can observe from outward expressions of words or behavior, while the majority under the surface consists of subconscious and unconscious motivating factors. Figure 5.3 (page 127) contains a fictional scenario that is meant to spark your thinking about how to tend to the social needs, self-image, traits, and motivations of the adult learners in the room. (See page 147 for a blank reproducible version of this figure.) The hypothetical situation is based on a high school social science department tasked with revising its curriculum and course of study to comply with state mandates that require culturally inclusive, accurate, and balanced perspectives from historically marginalized peoples. As you can see, this initiative spawns dissent, conflict, and discord within the team due to what's lurking beneath the surface of the water.

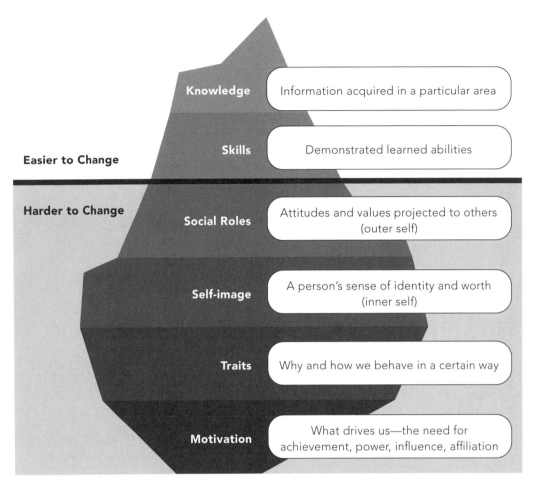

Easier to Change

Harder to Change

Knowledge	Information acquired in a particular area
Skills	Demonstrated learned abilities
Social Roles	Attitudes and values projected to others (outer self)
Self-image	A person's sense of identity and worth (inner self)
Traits	Why and how we behave in a certain way
Motivation	What drives us—the need for achievement, power, influence, affiliation

Source: Adapted from Noor Ismail et al., 2020.

Figure 5.2: Iceberg model of competencies.

While it is important to understand what can motivate colleagues and facilitators, it also benefits leaders to understand some of the underlying psychology that may impede progress during the planning stages of your initiative. *Impostor syndrome*—which is akin to *perfectionism, superheroism, uber-expertise*, or *lone wolf-ism*—is characterized as a general sense that all achievements a person has made have been unearned, accidental, or unjustified. This can inhibit any reasonable person's ability to accept new information and incorporate it into practice. Unfortunately, the *sage on the stage* persona is still alive and well in K–12 education. Letting go of the precept that you know what you are doing all the time takes courage and vulnerability, so any time that the leader or facilitator can model that *not knowingness* and lifelong learning is welcome and expected is worth its weight in gold. It encourages grace, growth, and generosity between and among participants.

Initiative: Adoption of revised K–12 culturally inclusive history and social science materials

Knowledge needed: Overview of new social science framework and pacing guides; how to revise existing lessons to incorporate new material; awareness of content that has been eliminated from outdated texts; connections to literature and English language arts standards

Skills required: Ways to conduct class discussion on sensitive topics; strategies for culturally responsive inclusion of minoritized groups; unconscious bias training; approaches to inquiry-based or thematic instruction in history, economics, government, sociology, and psychology courses

Self-image: Confronting one's own identity as a social science teacher; letting go of traditional or favorite modules, lessons, or projects that no longer fit or are appropriate; examining personally held beliefs and naming of one's own biases; feelings of loss, anger, inadequacy or being considered "wrong" for how one has taught history up until now

Social roles: Shifts in privilege or power between history department members (for example, the "old guard" losing power or influence to more progressive or social justice-centered teachers); women, LGBTQ+, and people of color gain status; potential rifts or alliances between colleagues based on personal or political belief systems

Motivation: Avoidance of looking ignorant; desire to be competent; maintenance of relationships; inclination to help and engage more students; meet supervision or evaluation goals; compliance

Traits: Resistance or reluctance to adopt new mindsets, theories, or pedagogy; fear of not knowing how to present new material effectively; loss or gain of expertise; overt rebellion or quiet refusal; blame or criticism directed at site or district administration for enacting changes

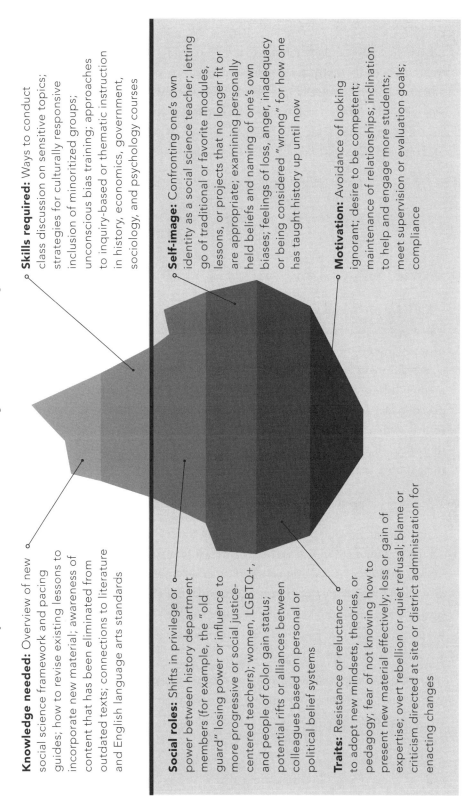

Figure 5.3: Iceberg model for professional learning design example.

CHANGE AND ADAPTATION

Change is hard, even when desired. It's a natural tendency for our fight-flight-freeze part of the brain to get clouded when confronted with new modes of operation. It may cause employees to worry about their job security, fear they will fail in the new environment, or lead to a climate of mistrust. Some employees may think "this is not what I signed up for!" In the face of resistance, Rebecca DuFour and Richard DuFour (2015) offer five tips for leaders:

- Assume good intentions.
- Identify specific behaviors essential to the success of the initiative.
- Focus on behavior, not attitude. Monitor behavior.
- Acknowledge and celebrate small victories.
- Confront incongruent behavior with specific concerns, and communicate logical consequences. (p. 8)

My advice: respond with compassionate firmness. We can't wait for people to warm up on their own to respond to centuries of delayed duty to educate historically disenfranchised students. Acknowledge the discomfort. Take the time to explain the *why*. And then get on with it. Change also takes time. It is incremental. It is formative. Just as with students learning new material that calls into question their own worldview or asks them to stretch beyond their comfort zone, so it is with adults. But the risks are much bigger. Educators are authorities in their field. They have earned advanced degrees and credentialing. They know their subject matter inside and out.

FACILITATION PREPARATION

Selecting an outside professional learning trainer can be beneficial to neutralize the playing field in cases where district insiders are associated with previous unpopular initiatives or bring with them other past baggage to overcome. Thus, in addition to carefully preparing the agenda and activities for the learning session, leaders must also meticulously pick the best facilitator they can possibly find, if they are not the person with the professional expertise or sufficient presentation skills themselves.

Best is a mutable term depending on collective personality of your district, the grade levels or content areas being addressed, or other unique qualities of the learners. One size does not fit all here. Teachers and administrators (present company included) are notoriously tough audiences to impress. And there are biases and predispositions that need be to overcome via intense planning before they've even walked in the room. So think about that *je ne sais quoi* of the person or people who can deliver the magical combination of the right energy and personality, legitimacy as a specialist, and skills and ability to win over the most challenging of crowds. A great training under your belt leads to a great launch in stage 9.

STAGE 9: LAUNCH

It's no small irony that, in my two books about the intricacies of launching new initiatives in schools and districts, the launch stage is, in many ways, quite straightforward. That's the point. This stage serves as a macrocosm of the previous eight microcosmic stages; since you've already learned a variety of tools, tested out theories in practice, and adequately prepared the field, all that's left is putting the whole process into action. The reason implementations have been so nerve-rattling in the past is likely because many leaders race through (or entirely skip) stages 1–6 to get to 7 and then cover stage 8 as an afterthought. Those days are over. Now you should feel calm, cool, and collected—with a dash of real excitement!

SMARTIE GOALS

I would venture to guess that there isn't a person in any industrialized country that hasn't heard of SMART goals. We've seen this cross-cutting concept across companies all over the world since at least 1981, when George T. Doran is believed to have coined the acronym. Since then, hundreds of variations of SMART goals have surfaced to serve the needs of various industries, teams, and individuals. A school leadership team version of this acronym developed by Anne E. Conzemius and Jan O'Neill (2014), founders of Quality Leadership by Design, includes five major elements.

1. **Strategic and specific:** "Strategic and specific means that these goals will have both broad-based and long-term impacts because they are focused on the specific needs of the students for whom the goal is intended." (p. 5)

2. **Measurable:** "Measurable means being able to know whether actions made the kind of difference we wanted: being able to measure a change in results because of those actions. Measurement can and should occur in a number of different ways using a variety of different tools and strategies." (p. 5)

3. **Attainable:** An "attainable [goal is] (within the realm of our influence or control) and doable (given current resources). To know whether a goal is attainable, you must know your starting point (baseline), how much time you have to accomplish the

goal, and what kinds of resources you have to make the necessary changes." (pp. 5–6)

4. **Results oriented:** A "results oriented [goal is] aimed at specific outcomes that schools can measure or observe. Results-oriented goals define not only what is expected but also desired as an end point." (p. 6)

5. **Time bound:** "Specifying a time frame for achieving the goal helps in two ways—first by providing a reference point for determining attainability, and second, by helping to keep the goal a priority . . . Having a time limit as part of a goal makes it imperative that we periodically check how well or swiftly we are progressing toward the goal." (p. 6)

During the mid-2010s, thought leaders improved upon the original by adding *inclusive* and *equitable* at the end of the first five letters to make *SMARTIE* goals (Swerdlow, 2019). With those two key additions, we are able to maximize impact as well as be more accountable for the students and families at the center of our initiatives. The two additional steps, inclusive and equitable, integrate into the SMART goal process as follows (Swerdlow, 2019).

6. **Inclusive:** Making a SMART goal inclusive involves sharing power in the design of processes, activities, decision making, and policymaking with traditionally excluded individuals or groups.

7. **Equitable:** An equitable goal is one that ensures everyone has the same opportunity to achieve the same outcomes by taking into account the historically marginalized identities that would otherwise hinder an individual or group's ability to do so.

While we are well past the goal-setting stage, the seven factors are still applicable to the implementation procedures you will be working on in this section. The Collaborative for Academic, Social, and Emotional Learning (CASEL; 2020) published a tool to help educators "prioritize clear, motivating goals for SEL" using SMARTIE examples and templates. These seven essential questions distill the major touchstones that we'll apply to the initiative implementation stage (CASEL, 2020). In your head, swap out the term *goal* with *execution* since you'll be using this to monitor and review your implementation midstream and execute any modifications needed as part of your continuous improvement process.

CASE STUDY

While not talked about in education circles as much as the homegrown equity issues right in our faces, the increase in people seeking asylum outside their country of origin has increased approximately 78 percent between 2011 to 2021, according to the United Nations High Commissioner for Refugees (2022) global trends report. "The number of people forced to flee due to persecution, conflict, violence, human rights violations and events seriously disturbing public order climbed to 89.3 million by the end of 2021" (p. 5). This should matter to equity-centered leaders because "41% of all forcibly displaced people are children [and] 48% of all refugee children remain out of school, and accessing education becomes harder as they get older" (Reid, 2023).

In a research study conducted by Sarah Dryden-Peterson, Elizabeth Adelman, Michelle J. Bellino, and Vidur Chopra (2019), the authors note:

> Inclusion in national schools [is] the foundation for access to quality education [as opposed to separate, but unequal schools reserved only for refugees], yet practices at national and school levels demonstrated a gulf between those aspirations and refugees' actual experiences of low-quality education. Contestation over whether and how refugee education was to enable belonging persisted at the school level, tightly aligned to understandings of what types of futures were possible for refugees [including the four possibilities of] resettlement, return, integration, and transnationalism . (pp. 356–357)

The authors also note the following:

> No matter the length of exile . . . [there is a] need for educational spaces that are free from exclusion and discrimination and for post-schooling opportunities that allow young people to use their education in pursuit of livelihoods and meaningful futures over the duration of exile and beyond. (Dryden-Peterson et al., 2019, p. 362)

Refugees, by definition, are fleeing unsafe, inhospitable, often life-threatening situations in their homelands, and often bring with them severe emotional and physical trauma that warrants immediate attention in the new country of residence schools. CASEL's (2020) simple yet profound model exemplified in figure 5.4 (page 132) is populated with responses relating to refugee or displaced students as the group needing special support.

STRATEGIC AND SPECIFIC What will change during Year 1, where, and for whom?	Students who are refugees or displaced from their home countries will be enrolled in a ten-session after-school program on each campus with critical mass (more than five students) to support their SEL needs and receive trauma counseling.
MEASURABLE What outcome measures or data sources should we use to measure success? What is a reasonable magnitude of the change that we should strive for?	Students will be given pre-, mid-, and post-surveys in their home language to compare their experiences of inclusion, belonging, and optimism from the beginning to the end of the ten sessions. We will also monitor attendance and discipline to gauge any increases or decreases, respectively. We can reasonably expect students to share reduced amounts of stress and other signs of trauma in one-on-one conversations with their counselors.
ATTAINABLE Given our current status and rate of progress toward what we want to accomplish during phase 1, what can we expect to achieve that is both ambitious and feasible?	The school has secured grants from the state government to implement SEL programming and from the federal government to serve refugee and displaced students. These two funding sources will allow us to pay for curriculum development and staff salaries, and acquire resources. The director of federal and state programs sanctioned the plan in August and has pledged ongoing support if the program is successful.
RESULTS ORIENTED Is this change clearly moving us closer to our shared vision for SEL and our school's overall strategic goals? How will we ensure this alignment is clear for our stakeholders?	There is no current program outside traditional academic supports to help displaced and refugee children in our district. We've developed a culturally responsive SEL curriculum specifically designed to address the kinds of trauma students have experienced in their home countries (primarily from Myanmar, Sudan, and Syria—the largest group of refugees in our enrollment) in order to help them recover and thrive in their new environment. With the new influx of refugees into our community, we will make clear to our stakeholders that it's in everyone's best interest to help newcomers feel welcome and able to navigate their new surroundings.

TIME BOUND	The curriculum was completed in October and instructors were hired in December to begin the series in January. After the ten sessions conclude in March, we will assess the program fully.
What is the time frame for this accomplishment, and when will there be checkpoints along the way?	
INCLUSIVE	This new SEL series will show students that there are caring adults they can connect with and rely on for support at school as they heal from trauma, learn to better manage complex emotions, and develop future-oriented mindsets. We will hold focus groups with them after the series is complete and ask participants for feedback on what was most beneficial and then hold co-planning meetings to develop a follow-up series.
As we later plan a series of action steps to accomplish this goal, how will we bring in traditionally excluded or marginalized groups to make decisions and contribute in a way that shares power?	
EQUITABLE	This program will be the first of its kind in our district. We have never specifically focused on refugee and displaced students in such a directed way. It will help students gain a sense of belonging and useful life skills and tools, whether they stay in our country, repatriate to their own, or resettle in another country.
Is this change clearly moving us toward greater equity in our school? In what ways will this address issues of injustice or oppression?	

Source: Adapted from CASEL, 2020.

Figure 5.4: Tool for developing SMARTIE goals for SEL.

*Visit **go.SolutionTree.com/diversityandequity** for a free reproducible version of this figure.*

THE IMPLEMENTATION ENGINE

In response to the massive $190 billion Elementary and Secondary School Emergency Relief (ESSER) funding infused into U.S. school districts in 2020, Chiefs for Change (2022) released a guidebook called *The Implementation Engine* to support district leaders in managing their new and competing resources. They underscore this chapter's caveats as they caution the following:

> A common implementation failure point is subjecting plans to insufficient review—both at the individual initiative level and across interdependent initiatives. This can hinder the ultimate impact and efficacy of an initiative. Even exciting initiatives that gain traction and launch quickly can ultimately fail to achieve their desired impact due to ineffective planning and insufficient pressure-testing of proposed plans. (Chiefs for Change, 2022, p. 30)

At any point in time, there are initiatives from the past, present, and future, all contending for a finite amount of space, resources, and attention. Even if the money is flowing—which is not very often an economic given in many states and countries—we can easily surpass our collective mental capacity before the physical bandwidth ever gives out. Furthermore, keep your eyes open for random initiatives generating from the inverted thinking of "We have $100,000, what can we buy?" rather than, "We have × number of prioritized equity gaps to close, what will it take to fully fund them?" Don't doubt that you will have colleagues who are not as equity focused as you are with their hands out for their piece of the pie. But if you come prepared with a plan, data to back it up, and a clear rationale for implementation, you'll have an advantage over those who still operate in that old way of thinking.

The Implementation Engine also includes a phase reflection worksheet (Chiefs for Change, 2022) from which the following prompts have been appropriated for stage 9 of the *Leading the Launch* process (Wallace, 2022). These prompts primarily involve data and accountability measures that a team should use as pre-planned progress checks during the first year of an implementation:

- Are the proposed metrics for measurement aligned with the system's strategic goals and priorities?
- Is there a clear path to collecting data to monitor and evaluate progress (e.g., baselines, midyear, and year-end targets)?
- Does this initiative include specific metrics to track impact across student groups?
- Can the initiative be linked to the existing accountability system?
- Is there potential for this initiative to exclude or negatively affect any specific student groups (or other stakeholder groups)?
- Have Year 1 targets been set? Are they informed by data? How do Year 1 targets connect to the longer-term initiative goals (e.g., multi-year targets)?
- Have clear milestones been identified (including milestones for stakeholder engagement, communication and training with staff, and monitoring and evaluation)? (Chiefs for Change, 2022, p. 55)

Extending beyond conventional information collection strategies, leaders should also include fewer formal and more on-the-ground observations and conversations with staff, students, and families involved in the initiative. Voice is a critical element in advancing equity for marginalized groups, so there should be ample opportunities for groups and individuals to share likes and dislikes, ask questions, and make suggestions. Some of the components from the resources mentioned earlier from CASEL (2020) and Chiefs for Change (2022) have been cross-referenced to develop this implementation inventory (see figure 5.5). (See page 148 for a blank reproducible version of this figure.)

Directions: This implementation inventory is intended to help leadership teams monitor and nurture the first year of a new initiative's lifespan. Combining the SMARTIE goal concept (CASEL 2020; Doran, 1981) with the Chiefs for Change (2022) checklist, add details from your own implementation plan in the right column.

SMARTIE Components	Implementation Checklist	Implementation Plan Features
STRATEGIC AND SPECIFIC What will change during Year 1, where, and for whom?	☐ Lead team members ☐ Staff involved ☐ Student groups affected ☐ Materials needed ☐ Locations ☐ How and when the rollout will take place	
MEASURABLE What outcome measures or data sources should we use to measure success? What is a reasonable magnitude of the change that we should strive for?	☐ Equity-centered standards to be met ☐ Metrics to track impact across student groups ☐ Baseline data collection ☐ Midyear targets ☐ End-of-year targets	
ATTAINABLE Given our current status and rate of progress toward what we want to accomplish during phase 1, what can we expect to achieve that is both ambitious and feasible?	☐ Links to existing accountability systems ☐ Access to current and necessary information ☐ Research-based evidence to support growth targets	
RESULTS ORIENTED Is this change clearly moving us closer to our shared vision for SEL and our school's overall strategic goals? How will we ensure this alignment is clear for our stakeholders?	☐ Problem of practice rationale ☐ Connections to existing implementations or other district programs ☐ Alignment with other equity-centered initiatives	

Figure 5.5: Implementation inventory.

continued ▶

SMARTIE Components	Implementation Checklist	Implementation Plan Features
TIME BOUND What is the time frame for this accomplishment, and when will there be checkpoints along the way	Dates or milestones for: ☐ Training and professional learning sessions ☐ Communications, outreach, and engagement ☐ Data collection, analysis, and reporting ☐ Board or community presentations	
INCLUSIVE As we later plan a series of action steps to accomplish this goal, how will we bring in traditionally excluded or marginalized groups to make decisions and contribute in a way that shares power?	☐ Leadership roles ☐ Feedback loop ☐ Input mechanisms ☐ Complaint resolution or remedy process	
EQUITABLE Is this change clearly moving us toward greater equity in our school? In what ways will this address issues of injustice or oppression	Systemic injustice to address: ☐ Reduction of first-, second-, and third-order barriers ☐ Expected learning, behavioral, and social outcomes ☐ Associated indicators impacted (for example, discipline, attendance, graduation, dropout rates)	

Source: Adapted from CASEL, 2020; Chiefs of Change, 2022; Doran, 1981.

Embedding predetermined benchmarks to keep track of the implementation throughout its first year will signal both a commitment to its success as well as empathic consideration for those immersed in it. It will not be perfect. While the pilot period in stage 4 may have exposed some flaws, others will inevitably arise during the implementation phase. However, these should not be inconceivable or jarring surprises—minor technical adjustments to the delivery plan and pivots are to be expected. Remember that this is a human endeavor and must be approached as such. When issues arise, we name them, share power in problem solving, and move forward with grace. You will learn a lot this first year and, with a continuous improvement mindset, shift into stage 10, which calls for ongoing support to fortify the initiative's well-being for the long term.

STAGE 10: SUSTAIN

This succinct definition by Helen Askell-Williams and Gloria A. Koh (2020) encapsulates stage 10: "Sustainable implementation is defined as the implementation of an effective initiative over a context-dependent timeframe leading to irreversible desirable system change" (p. 660). Sustained implementation is closely associated with a body of research tied to continuous improvement science. *Continuous improvement methodology* is construed of a series of steps that generally consist of some variation on the Plan-Do-Study-Act (PDSA) cycle, as W. Edwards Deming (2000) designed for the Japanese marketplace in 1951 and updated in 1993. The cycle attempts to answer three basic questions: (1) What are we trying to accomplish? (2) How will be know that a change is an improvement? and (3) What change can we make that will result in improvement? PDSA has evolved as a framework since then and continues to inform the field in different iterations, such as the one in table 5.1 from educational consultants Kim Bailey and Chris Jakicic's *Common Formative Assessment* (2012). PDSA "emphasizes and encourages the iterative learning process of deductive and inductive learning" in order to make systemic changes that make authentic impact on individuals in an organization (Moen & Norman, 2009, p. 10).

Table 5.1: Associates in process model for improvement.

	Guiding Questions	Team's Work and Products
Prepare	What norms should we follow to accomplish our team goals?	Group norms built through consensus and reviewed at least annually
Plan	What is our greatest area of need, and why? What is our action plan for addressing this need during the year? What does research say about how to improve? Is there something we're doing already that we can build on? What data should we collect along the way to monitor the change? Do we need to design a common formative assessment?	Analysis of data to determine the greatest area of need and development of a SMART goal (short or long term) Action plan that (1) addresses identified needs and outlines how to improve learning with specific steps to take and data to gather through formative and summative measures and (2) addresses how the team will implement plans, review results, and revise practices based on findings (such as with lesson study, observations, walkthroughs, and team feedback)

continued ▶

	Guiding Questions	Team's Work and Products
Do	How is the implementation of our plan going? Are we collecting data along the way? Do we need to learn more? Are we using agreed-on strategies and practices? Are any roadblocks interfering with our intervention or change in practice? How can we support each other? What resources can we use to support this implementation?	Implementing instruction as defined in the action plan, including common formative assessments Monitoring the implementation of new strategies Gathering interim data as defined in the action plan
Study	What has changed in our students' learning? Is the rate of change what we expected? More? Less? Are we leaving anyone behind? To what do we attribute these changes? Is there other data we want to gather?	Examine student work, results of common assessments, and other areas to determine the impact of actions on student learning. Determine other information that might be needed.
Act	Did we meet our goal? What did we learn throughout this process? What recommendations do we have for continuous improvement in this area? How can we hold the gains? What might be our next steps? How did we work together?	Determine any immediate actions or adjustments that are indicated (re-teaching, curricular adjustments, interventions). Develop recommendations for further work. Review group's performance (norms).

Source: Bailey & Jakicic, 2012, p. 98.

Asking these questions with an equity lens during this stage might look like the following.

- What are we trying to accomplish *to decrease performance gaps between student groups and increase learning outcomes for marginalized students?*

- How will we know that change is an improvement *for the student groups identified at the center of this implementation?*

- What changes can we make that will result in *the level of improvement desired for the next _____ months of the implementation?*

Continuous improvement feeds into Miia Sainio and colleagues' (2020) study in Finland on the implementation of an anti-bullying curriculum:

> Having active purveyors or agents promoting the program at school is important for sustainability. It is crucial to have a staff member or members who are in charge of the program coordination, especially with multicomponent programs with a whole-school approach to prevent and tackle bullying. (p. 140)

We will tap the basis of their research to depict a hypothetical scenario using the PDSA cycle as related to the bullying research conducted by Sainio's team (2020).

SCENARIO

A K–8 school district has implemented a new anti-bullying and character education program in its schools. The first unit is focused on reducing gender-based discrimination, name-calling, and stereotyping. The students took a baseline school climate assessment the first week of school, before the new program started. The PDSA cycle is applied via a follow-up climate survey during the fourth month of the school year to see what adjustments might need to be made.

1. **Plan:** What are your steps?

    We plan to administer surveys to students in grades 2, 4, 6, and 8 to learn how well the anti-bullying program is working to reduce gender biases and conflicts at school.

    We hope this produces data that shows students feeling safer and more included at school due to reduced incidences of gender-based assumptions, stereotyping, bullying, or harassment.

    We will:

    a. Create four age-appropriate surveys at the targeted grade level.

    b. Have students complete the surveys during advisory or homeroom period.

    c. Disaggregate the data by grade level to look for trends and produce a report of the findings

2. **Do:** What did you observe?

   We observed that students in grades 2 and 4 felt that the program was helping to stop name-calling and that gender equity was more evident in classroom procedures related to lining up, playground activities, and more balanced participation in class discussion. Grades 6 and 8 also reported fewer gender-based issues within the classroom setting but said that student interactions during after-school sports and unsupervised time (lunch, passing periods, and breaks) continue to be somewhat of a free-for-all for taunting and name-calling.

3. **Study:** What did you learn?

   Table 5.2 shows changes in student perceptions and experiences between the baseline survey and quarterly check-in.

   Analysis: Over the course of three months, feelings of school safety increased among all groups of students between 3–6 percent, with the largest increases in the elementary grades and to a lesser degree in the middle school years. For gender-based discrimination and bullying, decreases were observed across the board in both categories from 5–12 percent. While we are making incremental progress, we need to identify how the curriculum is productively impacting student behavior and where we need to redouble our efforts for the upcoming quarter.

4. **Act:** What are the next steps?

   We will:

   a. Review the newly adopted character education materials for specific lessons related to areas of concern indicated in the survey and implement those sections within the next three months

   b. Analyze disciplinary data to correlate whether there are changes in the number of referrals or suspensions related to gender-associated infractions or offenses

   c. Share data with teachers and ask for their ideas on strategies to address gender biases in the classroom as well as during students' unscheduled time

   d. Put a suggestion box near the counseling office for students to anonymously report concerns they personally experienced or situations they have witnessed that need to be addressed by staff

Table 5.2: Changes in Student Perceptions and Experiences

Survey Items Related to:	Second Grade	Fourth Grade	Sixth Grade	Eighth Grade
High levels of feeling safe and secure at school overall	Baseline: 88 percent Quarterly: 94 percent 6 percent increase	Baseline: 81 percent Quarterly: 88 percent 7 percent increase	Baseline: 74 percent Quarterly: 79 percent 5 percent increase	Baseline: 66 percent Quarterly: 69 percent 3 percent increase
Gender-related occurrences of bias or stereotyping	Baseline: 20 percent Quarterly: 10 percent 10 percent decrease	Baseline: 22 percent Quarterly: 10 percent 12 percent decrease	Baseline: 33 percent Quarterly: 25 percent 8 percent decrease	Baseline: 38 percent Quarterly: 32 percent 6 percent decrease
Gender-related incidents of bullying or harassment	Baseline: 8 percent Quarterly: 3 percent 5 percent decrease	Baseline: 16 percent Quarterly: 10 percent 6 percent decrease	Baseline: 22 percent Quarterly: 15 percent 7 percent decrease	Baseline: 31 percent Quarterly: 23 percent 8 percent decrease

You can conduct multiple PDSA cycles concurrently focusing on different strategies and data points or do them in serial fashion. They are meant to serve as thermometers to take the temperature of the implementation so you can make adaptations as a result. In the Darwinian world of school initiatives, it is truly the ability to be responsive to change and evolve accordingly that will generate longevity.

FIDELITY VERSUS INTEGRITY

Defining vague or overused terms like fidelity and integrity is especially important when it comes to linking them to equity-based initiatives. There are many hills already to climb when fighting for the rights of disenfranchised students, so you don't want to add to your challenge by using edu-speak that conjures up tainted or inaccurate associations. In their study on continuous improvement related to school-based implementations, Ariel Tichnor-Wagner and colleagues (2018) assert the following:

> When adaptations are promoted, the focus of evaluations is not on
> implementation fidelity, where the goal is to ensure that implementers

adhere closely to the innovation as "prescribed" and without modifications. Instead, the focus lies on what some in the educational-research
community have come to call implementation integrity. (p. 2)

This change in terminology is a welcome one as *fidelity* has, in many places, been weaponized against educators, especially in regard to formulaic curricular adoptions that insist upon lockstep movement from both teachers and students through a rigid pacing guide.

Integrity, on the other hand, is a more spacious concept that allows for personalization, decision making, and professionalism on the part of the implementer and the recipients. As long as the spirit behind the initiative clearly drives the details and choices are made in alignment with the stated intentions, variation is acceptable and even encouraged. In fact, Askell-Williams and Koh (2020) go one step further in their remarks that "If a system does not change to enable the client or student need to be satisfied, the initiative has not been successfully sustained" (p. 660). Therefore, we must continually let the initiative breathe and grow if it is to thrive, not merely survive.

As if that's not a weighty challenge enough, Leyton Schnellert (2020) warns that "when a school or district moves on to a new goal, the implementation of an innovative approach often becomes shallow or even abandoned due to a lack of investment or ownership on the part of teachers and school leaders" (p. 2). While you are simultaneously refining the implementation over the next several years, you are also contending with pending initiatives on the horizon that will command the spotlight. Shiny object syndrome is real; something in our human nature just can't resist newfangled things. When current initiatives eventually become older, it's easy for them to fade into the background. That is, unless we consciously keep them on the radar in fresh and bold ways. In figure 5.6, your charge is to purposefully find or invent structures to highlight the initiative's strengths and accomplishments and keep it in the limelight. (See page 150 for a blank reproducible version of this figure.)

In addition to the prepopulated events you've calendared, periodically tap recent research released on similar topics or seek out stories from the mainstream news media. You can set Google alerts with key words that will deliver new material to your inbox or bookmark websites that are designed to find articles on particular areas of interest. School safety, academic achievement (or lack thereof), mental health and social-emotional learning, student discipline, as well as controversial policies and social protests frequent the daily cycle so it shouldn't be difficult to draw those connections to your initiative and keep it on the radar. No matter whether the news item itself is positive or negative, you can craft favorable

Move around the prepopulated activities as relevant to your own setting, and add your own to the blank calendar (page 150) to help you map out awareness of the initiative throughout the school year. In addition to the traditional monthly activities schools and districts employ, think about how the following ideas might fit on the template to advance equity in the following unique ways.

- Tell student stories (blog posts, video diary, day in the life, website spotlights).

- Offer new incentives or rewards related to the initiative.

- Piggyback the initiative onto other newer initiatives, current events, or other pertinent situations.

- Create a lively challenge or contest related to the initiative.

- Invite families to special events to give the initiative a refreshed look (art show, performance, study trips).

School Year				
August–September	**October**	**November**	**December**	**January**
Welcome back newsletter in multiple languages	Multilingual monthly newsletter spotlighting a specific group's contribution at school	Multilingual monthly newsletter spotlighting a specific group's contribution at school	Multilingual monthly newsletter spotlighting a specific group's contribution at school	Multilingual monthly newsletter spotlighting a specific group's contribution at school
Updated student conduct policy including consequences for hate acts, harassment, and discrimination	Fall harvest festival: celebrate how different countries observe the change of seasons	Holiday or vacation messaging with information on accessing independent study for families extending travel to home countries	Human rights month highlighting refugee stories of triumph and persistence	Kindness challenge week with a focus on respect and inclusion for students with disabilities
Back-to-school kick-off events: Everyone Belongs Here! theme for diversity, equity, and inclusion	Bullying prevention month incorporating anti-discrimination resources for race, ethnicity, religion, gender, and disability	National American Indian and Alaskan Native heritage month guest speaker series	Winter break message related to different religious and cultural observances and festivities	100th day of school celebration: rally for school unity

Figure 5.6: Annual planning calendar.

continued ▶

February	March	April	May	June
Multilingual monthly newsletter spotlighting a specific group's contribution at school	Multilingual monthly newsletter spotlighting a specific group's contribution at school	Multilingual monthly newsletter spotlighting a specific group's contribution at school	Multilingual monthly newsletter spotlighting a specific group's contribution at school	End-of-school year newsletter thanking the school community for its diverse contributions
Graduate portraits showcase accessible to all parents and the community	Women's history month: female student art display in school libraries	Standardized assessments window messaging importance of stress management and mental health	Spring Carnival: worldwide expressions of dance, art, and music	LGBTQ+ pride month: raise rainbow flag at all sites and march in local parades
Black history month: inventors, innovators, and inspirations daily lessons	Spring break: post your pictures on our district social media page of you doing something fun, restful, or rejuvenating	Autism awareness month: strengths in our differences assembly and student performance	Asian American and Pacific Islander (AAPI) heritage month lunch and learns: The AAPI multiverse (our diverse national origins, languages, cultures, and religions)	Eighth grade promotion and high school graduation: decorate your mortarboard with symbols of self-love

associations to your implementation by framing the ways it is either bucking the (dispiriting) trends or riding the (progressive) successes. Many educators actively use social media to share interesting resources and promote best practices. Find some prolific posters or influencers who resonate with your own equity-centeredness and follow them to expand both your thinking and your network.

CONCLUSION

Bottom line: good going! Your hard-earned initiative implementation is now an essential part of the landscape of your organization. We've smoothed over the largest kinks, woven meaningful professional development throughout, and continually oriented new employees and students to the program, policy, or practice. From seed to sapling to tree, the ten-stage process is now complete. With the right amount of sun, water, and nourishment, it will grow stronger and become rooted, and in the best of all cases, provide a canopy of protection for future initiatives to come. But even good things must come to an end when the time is right, and chapter 6 (page 151) will address how to retire no longer blooming or fruit-bearing initiatives, particularly when vetted through an equity lens.

Professional Development Design Worksheet

Prompts for Key Features of Design: Team Response

Equity Lens

Describe how the specific equity problem of practice will be introduced and referenced throughout the staff learning experiences:

How we will leverage our own students' voices, experiences, and data to personalize the training and establish urgency:

How we will respond to deficit language, push-back, or refusal to acknowledge inequities exist in our system:

Iceberg Model for Professional Learning Design Template

Directions: Write the name of the initiative you are implementing that people need training or instruction on. Then evaluate the kinds of knowledge and skills that are expected or demonstrated above the waterline and then the variety of potential hidden motivators below the waterline that you will need to address overtly or covertly through high-quality professional learning design and delivery.

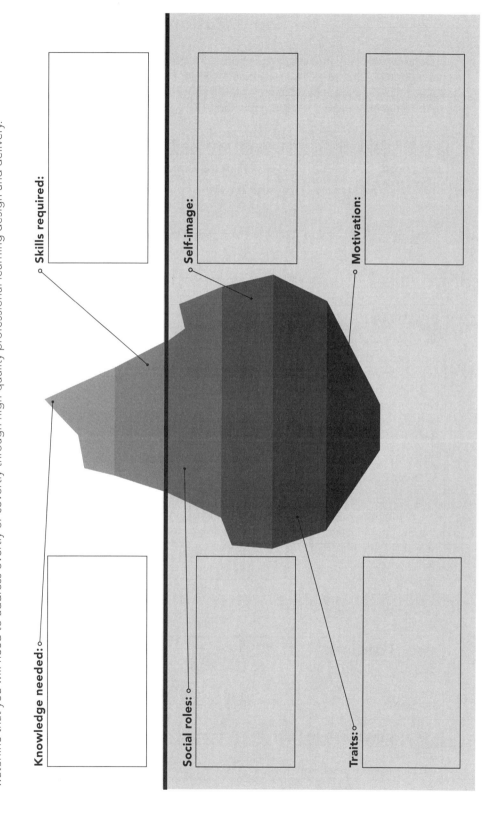

Skills required:

Knowledge needed:

Self-image:

Motivation:

Social roles:

Traits:

Implementation Inventory

Directions: This implementation inventory is intended to help leadership teams monitor and nurture the first year of a new initiative's lifespan. Combining the SMARTIE goal concept (CASEL, 2020; Doran, 1981) with the Chiefs for Change (2022) checklist, add details from your own implementation plan in the right column.

SMARTIE Components	Implementation Checklist	Implementation Plan Features
STRATEGIC AND SPECIFIC What will change during Year 1, where, and for whom?	☐ Lead team members ☐ Staff involved ☐ Student groups affected ☐ Materials needed ☐ Locations ☐ How and when the rollout will take place	
MEASURABLE What outcome measures or data sources should we use to measure success? What is a reasonable magnitude of the change that we should strive for?	☐ Equity-centered standards to be met ☐ Metrics to track impact across student groups ☐ Baseline data collection ☐ Midyear targets ☐ End-of-year targets	
ATTAINABLE Given our current status and rate of progress toward what we want to accomplish during phase 1, what can we expect to achieve that is both ambitious and feasible?	☐ Links to existing accountability systems ☐ Access to current and necessary information ☐ Research-based evidence to support growth targets	
RESULTS ORIENTED Is this change clearly moving us closer to our shared vision for SEL and our school's overall strategic goals? How will we ensure this alignment is clear for our stakeholders?	☐ Problem of practice rationale ☐ Connections to existing implementations or other district programs ☐ Alignment with other equity-centered initiatives	

SMARTIE Components	Implementation Checklist	Implementation Plan Features
TIME BOUND What is the time frame for this accomplishment, and when will there be checkpoints along the way?	Dates or milestones for: ☐ Training and professional learning sessions ☐ Communications, outreach, and engagement ☐ Data collection, analysis, and reporting ☐ Board or community presentations	
INCLUSIVE As we later plan a series of action steps to accomplish this goal, how will we bring in traditionally excluded or marginalized groups to make decisions and contribute in a way that shares power?	☐ Leadership roles ☐ Feedback loop ☐ Input mechanisms ☐ Complaint resolution or remedy process	
EQUITABLE Is this change clearly moving us toward greater equity in our school? In what ways will this address issues of injustice or oppression?	Systemic injustice to address: ☐ Reduction of first, second, and third-order barriers ☐ Expected learning, behavioral, and social outcomes ☐ Associated indicators impacted (for example, discipline, attendance, graduation, dropout rates)	

Source: Chiefs for Change. (2022, August). The implementation engine: A guidebook to support leaders from initiative planning to execution. *Washington, DC: Authors. Accessed at chiefsforchange.org/download-media/the-implementation-engine-a-guidebook-to-support-leaders-from-initiative-planning-to-execution on November 2, 2022.; Collaborative for Academic, Social, and Emotional Learning. (2020). Develop goals for Schoolwide SEL. Accessed at https://schoolguide.casel.org/resource/developing-goals-for-schoolwide-sel on November 2, 2022.; Doran, G. T. (1981). There's a S.M.A.R.T. way to write management's goals and objectives.* Management Review, 70(11), 35–36.

Annual Planning Calendar

School Year 20____–20____

August–September	October	November	December	January			

February	March	April	May	June			

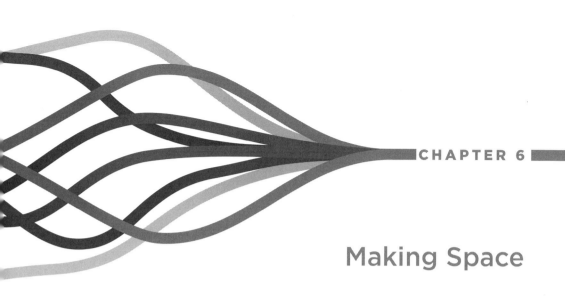

CHAPTER 6

Making Space

It cannot be repeated enough that we can't keep adding without taking away. *Leading the Launch* (Wallace, 2022) and this companion book grew from decades of personal and professional experience watching initiatives rise and fall. The first five chapters, without question, will help leaders quell the swell of current and proposed initiatives flowing into, through, and out of their organization. But there is another factor leaders must consider, which is where the space exists for a new initiative to thrive in the current environment.

I would be remiss not to give a nod to the elephant still taking up way too much space in the (class)room: *the COVID-19 pandemic*. Harvard researcher Fernando M. Reimers' (2022) analysis of primary and secondary education during COVID-19 exposes the following reality:

> The pandemic impacted education systems as they faced two serious interrelated preexisting challenges: educational inequality and insufficient relevance. A considerable growth in economic inequality, especially among individuals within the same nations, has resulted in challenges of social inclusion and legitimacy of the social contract, particularly in democratic societies. (p. 11)

In concert with Reimers' (2022) observations, in her testimony before the U.S. House of Representatives Committee on Education and Labor on June 22, 2020, Valerie Wilson from the Economic Policy Institute proclaimed:

> Although the current strain of the coronavirus is one that humans have never experienced before, the disparate racial impact of the virus is deeply rooted in historic and ongoing social and economic injustices. Persistent racial disparities in health status, access to health

care, wealth, employment, wages, housing, income, and poverty
all contribute to greater susceptibility to the virus—both economi-
cally and physically.

These two quotations are at the crux of why I felt this book needed to be written as a corollary to my first. It is not enough to teach leaders how to implement
school and district initiatives, writ large, with the (now much more obvious to me)
serious fissures of structural inequities the pandemic stripped bare. Introducing
new programs or projects that protect the already privileged or further widen the
opportunity gaps between the haves and the have-nots is just plain wrong. And
I needed to rectify the potential that benign harm could be committed with my
earlier work.

When "things fall apart," as William Butler Yeats (1919/2008) lamented in the
wake of World War I (1914–1918) and during the Great Influenza pandemic
(1918–1920) that wiped out nearly 100 million people between them, "the center
cannot hold" (p. 188). That center today is educating in ways that are incongruent with the future we hope to engineer. While Yeats' (1919/2008) poem from
which those lines have been lifted, "The Second Coming" is hardly consoling, it
contains a glimmer of hope that out of the wreckage a new epoch will rise.

Poetry aside, the social contract that Reimers (2022) referenced and the Age
of Enlightenment (1685–1815) philosophers Jean Jacques Rousseau, Thomas
Hobbes, and John Locke all attempted to characterize essentially boils down
to the relationship between individuals and their degree of responsibility to the
greater whole while also maintaining their own free will. Rather than debating
whether and how our various social compacts over the past 400 years have been
actualized or thwarted, I prefer to adopt UNESCO's International Commission
on the Futures of Education's call to action in their 2021 report and embrace my
role in the Zeitgeist. In the report, titled "Reimagining Our Futures Together,"
they assert:

> Education can be seen in terms of a social contract—an implicit agree-
> ment among members of a society to cooperate for shared benefit. A
> social contract is more than a transaction as it reflects norms, commit-
> ments and principles that are formally legislated as well as culturally
> embedded. . . . As we face grave risks to the future of humanity and
> the living planet itself, we must urgently reinvent education to help us
> address common challenges. This act of **reimagining means work-
> ing together to create futures that are shared and interdependent**.
> The new social contract for education must unite us around collec-
> tive endeavors and provide the knowledge and innovation needed

to shape sustainable and peaceful futures for all anchored in social,
economic and environmental justice. (p. 2)

Coming out of the COVID-19 pandemic, during which we saw innumerable
new initiatives in schools, Justin Reich (2022) proffers:

What if we started, not with addition, but with subtraction? Make
school simpler. Give teachers and students room to breathe. Clear out
the marginal and focus on the most important things. When people
feel a little lighter, then figure out what your schools are missing and
what to strategically add to make them stronger.

Education has always been a tough gig, but few of us truly foresaw the utter
upheaval wrought by two-plus years of intense and then lingering pandemic
conditions, conditions that will likely have a permanent impact on how schools
operate for the next generation of both students and educators. If we want to
have an influence on that future, subtraction is essential.

So while this chapter is technically outside the ten-stage process, without an eye
toward making space for new initiatives to succeed, you're still stuck in a bind.
Alas, there are no clean slates. No matter when you enter the leadership ranks of
a school, district, county office, or state department of education, there are, and
will be, implementations that came before. And, in many cases, they linger long
beyond what should be their natural shelf life. If left to linger, overload, burnout, and disengagement are waiting in the wings. Luckily, there are steps we can
take to avoid reaching that point. In this chapter, we'll look at the consequences
of initiative overload, methods for preventing initiative burnout, review a low-
cost high-impact scenario, and learn how to perform an equity audit.

INITIATIVE OVERLOAD

At the basest level, initiative overload occurs when leaders at all levels in the
organization have an unrestricted ability to select, purchase, and carry out any
new enterprise they want, from principals buying new instructional tools without
going through the curriculum and instruction department and human resources
adding new layers of bureaucracy without considering the impact on users to
technology services changing website hosting but neglecting to notify staff that
their individual pages would no longer be supported. The degree to which these
kinds of unregulated activities are permissible via a *blank check* mentality have
impacts that range from mild annoyance at the supposed upgrade to totally
untenable circumstances for staff and students who are typically the ones who
bear the brunt of too many obligations and changes to keep up with at once.

Not to mention, the lack of process jeopardizes what could be a worthy equity-centered initiative's longevity and success, but instead causes it to be suffocated by the surrounding chaos.

And so, leaders are often in a position where they must take a step back to reassess the viability of what's already in place. In *Leading the Launch*, the "Initiative Assessment Tool" broaches the topic of eliminating no longer productive initiatives (Wallace, 2022, p. 154). You may want to select one school or division before taking on the entire district, ministry, county office, or department of education, which could land you in a paralyzing quagmire. Rely on the data at your disposal that's been hinting (or screaming) that a program is not serving marginalized segments of your student population in fundamental ways. Then, for each criteria under the guiding questions, evaluate the program from low or negative impact (1) to highly effective at reducing inequities (5). This exercise, in figure 6.1, will help set the context for the rest of this chapter in its revised equity-centered format for program evaluation. (See page 172 for a blank reproducible version of this figure.)

While this rating system will help the leadership team quantify the higher- and lower-ranked implementations, it will not suffice by itself to determine the future. Much like adopting new initiatives, this winnowing process also needs to have research backing the recommendation, ample stakeholder engagement, data or evidence that show a lack of impact or influence, and clear steps for sunsetting the no longer effective program, policy, or practice.

Rose Hollister and Michael D. Watkins's (2018) article in the *Harvard Business Review* asserts that seven variables contribute to initiative overload in the business world. The categories are remarkably like what we see in the education realm. The terms Hollister and Watkins (2018) coin mostly remain intact, but I've added my own descriptors to show how each plays out in our field. The seven variables are as follows.

1. **Impact blindness:** Inability to track or count how many total initiatives are impacting the entire system and how they either aid or impair historically marginalized students' educational experiences

2. **Multiplier effects:** A lack of or a limited view of how many initiatives are being generated from different district office departments or from the senior leadership team into the rest of the organization, and that may be disproportionately serving or ignoring various demographics

Directions: The guiding questions are linked to the point values assigned to each item in assessing how close the program, product, or service is to meeting school or district equity-centered goals. For ease of phrasing, the generic term *implementation* will be used but is meant to be replaced with more specific descriptors such as *master scheduling, physical education standards, robotics program, SEL curriculum, zero waste project,* and so on. Rate each criterion to arrive at a total score.

Implementation: *[Add details here]*

Guiding Questions	Rating Scale (low to high)				
1. Is the implementation, as it stands, strategically aligned to the most recent versions of equity-centered district plans?	1	2	3	4	5
2. Is the implementation making a direct and measurable impact on the intended student groups?	1	2	3	4	5
3. Has the implementation helped to close performance gaps between identified student groups?	1	2	3	4	5
4. How well does the implementation connect to or advance other concurrent equity-centered initiatives?	1	2	3	4	5
5. Does the implementation have support from the students, families, and staff it is meant to serve?	1	2	3	4	5
6. Is the implementation still relevant and meaningful for 21st century learning and diverse postsecondary college and career readiness?	1	2	3	4	5
7. Do the contributions to educational equity justify the level of investment or resources to keep it up to date?	1	2	3	4	5
8. Is the implementation (still) required by law or moral obligation to marginalized students?	1	2	3	4	5
9. Do we have a superior implementation to fill its prior role in the organization?	1	2	3	4	5
10. If eliminated, how intense would the opposition to its removal be by minority groups who might retain benefits from it?	1	2	3	4	5
Scoring Guide: 10–24 points: Eliminate the implementation. 25–39 points: Conduct more outreach and reevaluate. 40–50 points: Keep the implementation.	Total:				

Source: Adapted from Wallace, 2022.

Figure 6.1: Equity-focused initiative assessment tool.

3. **Political logrolling:** Favors, pet projects, or vested interests by outside players in the community that gain support in exchange for some other service or fulfillment of a promise (see also: bartering, bargaining, quid pro quo, glad-handing), especially ones that foment privilege and favoritism toward those in power

4. **Unfunded mandates:** A governing body such as the state or federal legislature passes a law but does not allocate any (or sustained) funding to implement the now-required initiative; while often intended to reduce gaps or rectify injustices, it can fall by the wayside once the money's gone.

5. **Bandage initiatives:** Well-intentioned but superficial solutions that don't adequately get at the root of the problem of practice leadership is attempting to solve; this includes performative gestures that have no action tied to them, like requiring everyone to post their pronouns on their email signatures as your entire LGBTQ+ visibility campaign or passing board resolutions that only symbolically lend support to minoritized populations (like National Two Different Colored Shoes Day or Sikh Awareness Month).

6. **Cost myopia:** Failing to plan a multiyear budget with consideration to the ebb and flow of financial trends or to have alternative funding sources lined up; during lean budget years, eliminating staff positions, materials, or needed resources but not cutting the amount of work expected to deliver the initiative. The low-hanging fruit of perceived extra services and support staff (like parent liaison coordinators or diversity, equity, inclusion managers) that primarily exist to help underrepresented families or personnel in the district, end up first to go.

7. **Initiative inertia:** Habits, infrastructure, comfort, lack of will, unchallenged rationales, "if it ain't broke, don't fix it" mentalities, and other protectors of the status quo that continue to subjugate those lacking such stature in the organization

Table 6.1 also provides concrete examples of each category in the right column to illustrate when and how each might materialize in a school district.

Table 6.1: Seven Causes of Initiative Overload

Causes of Initiative Overload	Education-Based Examples
1. Impact blindness: Inability to track or count how many total initiatives are impacting the entire system and how they either aid or impair historically marginalized students' educational experiences	The district has sanctioned and supports one official classroom management system that has been vetted and determined to be the most compliant product related to accessibility laws, but teachers all over the district have downloaded other programs and apps without seeking permission from the instructional technology department. There is no mechanism for finding out how many other classroom management platforms are in use, how they are being used and with whom, the toll on the internet infrastructure, or if they meet the legal standards for student with IEPs or 504 Plans.
2. Multiplier effects: A lack of or a limited view of how many initiatives are being generated from different district office departments or from the senior leadership team into the rest of the organization, and that may be disproportionately serving or ignoring various demographics	This fall, the human resources department is embarking on a document scanning project to digitize all personnel files. Curriculum and instruction are moving from hard copy to online textbooks in all core subject areas. Student services are shifting from paper-based enrollment to an online portal; all the while, technology services are adding stricter cybersecurity measures that may seriously impede (or completely tank) these affiliated technological efforts. Furthermore, no one has checked to see how any of these shifts from paper-based to digital modalities may further marginalize students and families without sufficient access to technology or the internet.
3. Political logrolling: Favors, pet projects, or vested interests by outside players in the community that gain support in exchange for some other service or fulfillment of a promise (see also: bartering, bargaining, quid pro quo, glad-handing), especially ones that foment privilege and favoritism toward those in power	A school board member is heavily involved in a community organization working on a grant to bring in funding for a global climate change awareness project. The nonprofit's chances of receiving the grant award increases exponentially if they partner with a public school district. The trustee pressures the superintendent to place the grant partnership on the board agenda for a vote, even though the district already has a program that more intentionally focuses on how climate change impacts socioeconomically disadvantaged peoples and racial minorities plus makes advancing equity a more prominent feature in the curriculum.

continued ▶

Causes of Initiative Overload	Education-Based Examples
4. Unfunded mandates: A governing body such as the state or federal legislature passes a law but does not allocate any (or sustained) funding to implement the now-required initiative; while often intended to reduce gaps or rectify injustices, it can fall by the wayside once the money's gone	A state legislature passes a dyslexia screening mandate that all school districts must adopt, including purchasing licenses for a pricey accredited assessment and providing staff training to administer, download, and interpret test results. School districts are expected to tap already overextended special education budget lines to pay for the implementation—and have no resources allocated to provide interventions for students whose screens come back as conclusive for the disorder.
5. Bandage initiatives: Well-intentioned but superficial solutions that don't adequately get at the root of the problem of practice leadership is attempting to solve, including performative gestures or impotent resolutions	Employee wellness is a significant concern coming out of the pandemic. A county office of education brokers a deal with local gyms to offer free memberships to any of its staff for six months in an attempt to boost health and fitness. Forgetting that more than 60 percent of their staff live outside the district's boundaries, thus making the gyms inconvenient, only 18 percent can take advantage of the program, and it does little to unearth (or resolve) the complex conditions truly influencing depleted levels of employee satisfaction in the organization.
6. Cost myopia: Failing to plan a multiyear budget with consideration to the ebb and flow of financial trends or to have alternative funding sources lined up; during lean budget years, eliminating staff positions, materials, or needed resources but not cutting the amount of work expected to deliver the initiative	To mitigate rising fuel costs, the district swaps out its gasoline-powered fleet of buses with electric vehicles, subsidized by a government rebate program. In three years, the local electricity company increases rates by 25 percent to cover its own costs of doing business. The rebate ends, and the district cannot find enough qualified bus drivers that live nearby due to a housing price boom. When budget cuts hit, the transportation program is eliminated entirely, leaving dozens of nearly new and empty buses languishing in the yard. And, more importantly, leaves hundreds of low-income and rural students without adequate transportation.
7. Initiative inertia: Habits, infrastructure, comfort, lack of will, unchallenged rationales, "if it isn't broken, don't fix it" mentalities, and other protectors of the status quo that continue to subjugate those lacking such stature in the organization	Every school in the district has traditionally hosted a back-to-school night in the fall and an open house in the spring. There have been no adjustments in the format, schedule, or content regardless of whether anyone—students, parents, or staff—gets any value or satisfaction out of the events. The two events have become something to be endured rather than enjoyed. But whenever the issue is raised to update the structure, objectives, or activities to make the events more vibrant, multicultural, or reflective of the community demographics, nothing much happens.

Source: Adapted from Hollister & Watkins, 2018.

Some of the scenarios in table 6.1 (page 157) probably sound familiar to you. Even if not, reasonable people must be shaking their head, thinking *what a waste*. Of time. Of effort. Of ingenuity. Of morale. And, of course, of money. Keep all of these in mind as we head into the next section.

WASTE REDUCTION

Preventing initiative overload is possible. And if we're being truly honest, it's a moral, fiscal, and operational imperative. Schools are not businesses. We don't produce widgets or make profits, but we do have to manage our resources, balance our budgets, and make proper use of the funding apportioned to us through local, state, and federal means. This section is not a master class on school finance but rather a short treatise on waste reduction.

As of 2022, K–12 schools in the United States spend an average of $16,993 per student annually, although each state varies widely in its expenditures, from Idaho at the lowest end at $8,041 to the District of Columbia topping $22,832 (Hanson, 2022b). Think of all the millions, if not billions, of dollars that have been lost to aborted and failed initiatives over the past century. National research director at the Thomas B. Fordham Institute Adam Tyner observes in the perpetual economics versus outcomes debate, "Typically, what policymakers and administrators need to know is not whether money makes a difference, but what the relationship between money and school performance looks like—and what uses of money make what kinds of differences in performance" (as cited in Hess & Wright, 2020, p. 42). That's what we intend to do here through the next series of exercises.

There's more than one way to peel a banana, and you have to decide which approaches will best get you there. It's important to mention up front that U.S. school districts spend, on average, 80 percent of their budgets on personnel salary and benefits, so when you cut programs, you're almost always also cutting people (National Center for Education Statistics [NCES], 2022). Eliminating jobs is never easy (and sometimes near impossible depending on union contract clauses), but the blows can be cushioned by creating new positions that directly serve our students who are most in need. So anytime you need to retire an implementation, consider how you can creatively reallocate your human resources at the same time.

Reich (2022) states:

> The cost of having overly complex systems weighs heavily on all of us, but each individual element imposes only modest costs of time, energy, and attention to lots of people in the system, while offering

> benefits to small, determined groups of stakeholders . . . [thus result-
> ing in] a hodge-podge of priorities and initiatives.

We need objective tools to level the playing field because emphasizing the myriad benefits that privilege some groups may cause us to overlook those with the identified needs.

Leading the Launch includes a cost-to-impact matrix in the prioritization stage (Wallace, 2022). This grid is a practical instrument for weighing the financial pros and cons of services, plans, processes, or products your district has already implemented. It offers leaders a rudimentary look at the initiatives all on a single page to see "what uses of money make what kinds of differences in performance" (as cited in Hess & Wright, 2020, p. 42). Using the tool in figure 6.2, your team will list everything that's on the table for discussion in order to exact a long-range view of effectiveness. (See page 173 for a blank reproducible version of this figure.) Your list will inform your work going into the discrete process of making recommendations described next. Before you begin to fill out the matrix, you'll need to gather a minimum of two data points for each initiative you plan to deconstruct: (1) total costs including staffing, resources, materials, training, salaries, and so on, and (2) valid data to show progress, achievement, or targeted outcomes met by identified groups of historically underserved students in your schools. Then your team will come to consensus before listing each initiative in the most appropriate box. The items that land in low impact quadrants (1 and 2) are candidates for elimination during the next part of the retirement process.

In the examples in figure 6.2, here are some brief explanations for why each was categorized in one of the four quadrants:

- **Quadrant 1 (low cost and low impact):** One-and-done motivational assemblies are relatively inexpensive, but don't show lasting impacts on student behavior or academic efforts.

- **Quadrant 2 (high cost and low impact):.** SMART Boards in every classroom may provide equitable technologies, but not if teachers each get to decide on their own whether to use them to their full capacity.

- **Quadrant 3 (high cost and high impact):** Instructional coaches that have been trained in culturally competent practices have a widespread impact on the teachers they coach and model lessons that can transform instruction districtwide.

- **Quadrant 4 (low cost and high impact):** Hosting practical life skills workshops, staffed by volunteer experts from the community, have been highly engaging and well-attended and students report they frequently use the information they learn.

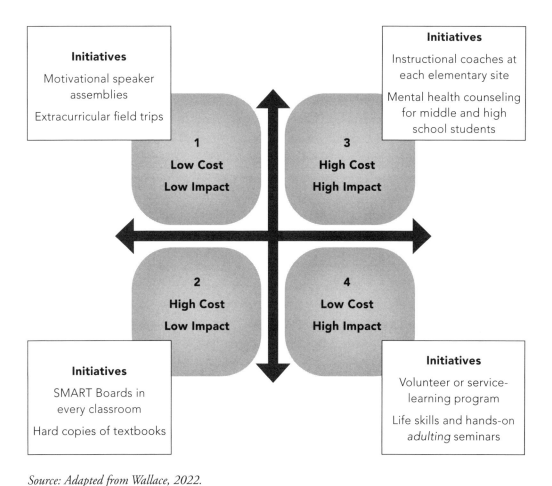

Source: Adapted from Wallace, 2022.

Figure 6.2: Cost-impact matrix.

Let's take a deeper dive into one hypothetical low-cost, high-impact scenario. Through the cost-impact matrix exercise, a high school's leadership team has uncovered certain test scheduling practices that are negatively impacting neurodivergent—those who are on the autism spectrum or have attention deficit hyperactive disorder (ADHD)—students' ability to focus consistently enough to perform accurately on standardized assessments. In accordance with Tracey Burns's (2017) research, many countries:

> Require . . . young people with special learning needs [to] participate in similar academic assessments to their peers (OECD, 2016), with perhaps some modification depending on the severity of their disorder. An ongoing issue in neurodiversity research and practice is how to assess students without subjecting them to uncomfortable environments or activities that may not accommodate their needs and skills. (p. 5)

The leadership team decides to take on the historical testing schedule employed each spring to accomplish the 95 percent participation rate required by the state or province department of education.

At this point, there is the aforementioned need to enter a process of making recommendations, so the dean of instruction pulls together a task force of students, parents, special educators, regular classroom teachers, and school counselors and administrators to codesign a new model to more equitably accommodate students with learning and processing differences. The task force discovers that shifting the schedule from the original model to the new design, illustrated in figure 6.3, would not only improve the assessment experience for neurodivergent learners but also positively affect other student groups and benefit the overall school climate.

Flexibility. Choice. Individualization. Frequent breaks. High-interest activities. Enthusiasm. These are not concepts usually associated with compliance-driven standardized testing. Counterweighing the seriousness of the assessments with social, personalized, and enjoyable school activities helps shift student and staff mindsets, resulting in better stress management, increased focus, and elevated mood. The school's leadership team looks forward to evaluating whether these novel conditions will translate to higher outcomes for the neurodivergent students at the center of their focus.

RETIREMENT PLANNING

Don't get too excited—it's not your retirement! We need you need to stick around a while longer to see things through. I'm talking about retiring old initiatives that have overstayed their welcome and should now be gently put away. Some will not be missed, while others might raise alarms. The examples supplied in *Leading the Launch* are worth recounting here (with the overlay of equity prompts) for vetting purposes in table 6.2 (page 164). (See page 175 for a blank reproducible version of this table.)

> Not all initiatives that face elimination should be replaced with anything at all. We must also question the policies, historical practices, traditions, and instructional activities. . . . This is not to say that any of the practices in the list are right or wrong, but that it's valuable to examine whether they are perpetuating systems that hurt more than help students. (Wallace, 2022, p. 151)

Traditional Testing Schedule (three consecutive days)			
8:10 a.m.–12:00 p.m.	English Language Arts, Parts 1 and 2	Mathematics, Parts 1 and 2	Science and Social Science
12:01 p.m.–12:36 p.m.	Lunch	Lunch	Lunch
12:40 p.m.–1:40 p.m.	Period 1	Period 3	Period 5
1:45 p.m.–2:45 p.m.	Period 2	Period 4	Period 6

Reimagined Testing Schedule (one day a week over the course of three weeks)			
8:10 a.m.–8:40 a.m.	Focus on Wellness: Strategies for Calming and Centering	Focus on Wellness: Problem Solving and Conflict Resolution	Focus on Wellness: Sleep and Nutrition Routines
8:45 a.m.–10:15 a.m.	English Language Arts, Part 1	Mathematics, Part I	Science
10:15 a.m.–10:25 a.m.	Nutrition Break	Nutrition Break	Nutrition Break
10:30 a.m.–12:00 p.m.	Mathematics, Part 2	Social Science	English Language Arts, Part 2
12:00 p.m.–12:40 p.m.	Lunch	Lunch	Lunch
12:45 p.m.–2:45 p.m.	*Student Choice:* • Library or Study Hall • Physical Education or Field Sports • Improv Theater • Music Circle • Art Therapy	*Tutorials:* Student may select up to four of their six classes to check in for homework help, make up assignments, or get extra support in thirty-minute rotations	*Spring Fling Activities:* • Pep Rally • Club Booths • Robotics Demos • Dance Team Showcase • Games and Contests

Figure 6.3: Traditional and reimagined assessment schedules.

Table 6.2: Equity Vetting of Legacy Practices.

Long-term Educational Practices	Vetting for Educational Equity Efficacy
Instructional: Homework, test prep, copying down lecture notes, rote memorization, filling in worksheets, repetition	• Is the instructional practice still benefiting diverse groups of students? How do you know? • Is the practice supported by progressive and conclusive educational research? • Will the practice help develop college and career skills and key competencies that marginalized students will need for their postsecondary future?
Assessment: Pop quizzes, weighted grades, zeros for not completing assignments, red ink, standardized testing, report cards, A–F grading	• Does the practice motivate all students to improve or discourage some non-dominant groups' progress? • Has the practice disproportionately negatively impacted specific demographics of students? If so, which groups and why? • Is the practice a realistic, reliable, and valid means of assessing what students know and can do? Does it favor certain groups over others?
Disciplinary: Suspensions for truancy, recess detention, dress codes or school uniforms, zero tolerance for drugs or violence, cell phone bans, Saturday school	• Do the data show discrepancies in application of the policy to different students by race, gender, language, socioeconomics, special needs, or cultural background? Describe how. • Does the practice inspire behavioral changes or increased self-discipline equivalently among and between all student groups? • Are the practices the best alternatives the school can employ to improve school climate, culture, and safety? Including for historically disenfranchised students?
Organizational: Bell schedules, busing, hall passes, bathroom permissions, school start and end times, desks in rows	• Is there a solid rationale and explanation for the practice? Does the mechanism still function reasonably well for today's students from all backgrounds? • Do students across the district experience the same benefits (or penalties) of the practice? • Does the practice affect different segments of the school population fairly? Does it work?

Traditions: Science fairs, spelling bees, talent contests, pep rallies, assemblies, school rivalries, homecoming court	• Is the practice primarily a White, heteronormative legacy that lacks relevance to non-White, non-straight pupils? • How do students of color, racial minorities, linguistically diverse, and LGBTQ+ students tend to fare in these competitions? • Does the practice encourage unity or create greater divisions between student groups?
Stratification: Ability grouping; academic (basic, college prep, honors) and vocational tracking; retention for failure; gifted and talented education; special education; language, racial, and social inequities; class rankings	• When disaggregating the data, are minoritized students equitably represented in the advanced learning environments or relegated to lower-track paths? • Is the practice necessary to comply with higher education admission criteria or workplace employment or are there alternative measures that can be leveraged instead? • What are the short- and long-term effects or consequences of maintaining the practice on marginalized students?

As in stage 1 of the ten-stage process, the questions in table 6.2 are designed to send your team back to the drawing board to research, investigate, and probe the efficacy of practices that were long ago woven into the fabric of your school or district. Efficacy, in this case, must be viewed through the perspective of equity with the essential question being: *Does this practice support marginalized students' growth, capacities, or proficiencies at school and beyond?* If the answer is no, or even maybe, it's our responsibility to cross-examine the curriculum, measurement tool, rule, procedure, policy, custom, or routine to unmask, interrogate, and remedy the underlying issues.

Looking back to the introduction of this book (page 5), *equity-centered initiatives* were defined as having one or a combination of the following six factors.

1. New to the K–12 field or has not yet been tried in your school or district to reduce barriers or improve conditions for historically marginalized students

2. Currently exist, but significant changes are being considered to refocus the work toward educational equity

3. Deliberate research-based approaches that benefit specifically identified groups of families, students, or staff

4. Require resources above and beyond what may be currently budgeted or planned for, but are worth seeking out to level the playing field

5. An immediate response to emerging needs or changing conditions that lend opportunities for increasing equitable conditions

6. Generated from school sites, governing board, business services, human resources, instructional services, or outside entities (government, legal system, community groups) as a call to right a wrong or take social justice action on behalf of a minoritized group

We are now going to flip these six items to see how you can uproot ineffectual, detrimental, or wasteful initiatives from your organization. The inverse of equity-centered initiatives will be designated as *equity-obstructive* programming and may include any of these hallmarks.

1. Pervasive throughout the K–12 field or endemic in your school or district and that maintain barriers or create impediments for historically marginalized students

2. Currently exists, but significant changes are being considered that may intentionally or unintentionally hamper educational equity

3. Widespread, large-scale, all-student or whole-school programs that may neutrally or negatively impact specific groups of families, students, or staff

4. Requires budgeting and resources for maintaining prevailing implementations, sometimes coupled with refusal to reallocate funding for equity purposes

5. A kneejerk reaction to emerging needs or changing conditions that may cause, perpetuate, or exacerbate inequities in the system

6. Generated from school sites, governing boards, business services, human resources, instructional services, or outside entities (government, legal system, community groups) to protect privileged stakeholders, uphold the status quo, and conserve power structures

In a spirit of generosity, let's give the benefit of the doubt to our forebears who likely believed their past initiatives were doing a good service to students. Remember, much of what we may now consider archaic was probably considered cutting-edge and pioneering at the time. Educators are generally a well-intentioned lot. Very few (and ideally none) go into the profession actively seeking to do damage. But once we know better, we must do better. Figure 6.4 is your entry into arbitrating between the good, the bad, and the in-between. (See page 174 for a blank reproducible version of this figure.) It's time to take a fresh look at older initiatives in your organization to analyze whether they should remain, are able to be optimized for inclusion and equity of marginalized groups, or should be recommended for an overdue retirement. Here, your team will list any existing implementation from quadrants 1 and 2 from the "Cost-Impact Matrix" reproducible (page 173) to be dissected to determine its future in your district.

Existing Initiative Implementation	Cost-to-Impact Ratio	Opportunities for Inclusion and Equity Focus	Recommendation to Superintendent or Governing Body
Over 80 percent of core novels required in secondary English classes are written by White American or European males from privileged backgrounds.	Low cost, low impact: financially Novels have already been purchased, so the costs are negligible. However, the low impact is extremely concerning as the existing canon does not represent or engage 85 percent of our student population.	Assemble a curriculum committee of students, parents, and teachers to read and recommend new titles by all-gendered authors of diverse ethnic, linguistic, racial, and cultural backgrounds, with the goal of 50 percent or higher representation.	☐ Keep as is. ☑ Revise for inclusion and equity. ☐ Propose retirement.
Recess or lunch detention used as elementary school classroom management or discipline techniques for misbehaviors.	High cost, low impact: socioemotionally It costs nothing financially, but the practice is demoralizing and unhealthy for student well-being and does not mitigate problem behaviors.	Students need breaks to expend energy, get fresh air and exercise, socialize with peers, and have enough time to eat. This punitive practice needs to be eliminated and totally replaced with positive behavioral supports.	☐ Keep as is. ☐ Revise for inclusion and equity. ☑ Propose retirement.

Figure 6.4: Implementation inspection.

EQUITY AUDIT

If you don't have enough information to make a clear recommendation to the superintendent or governing body, conducting an equity audit of the program or practice you want to investigate could help. This is especially true if you are delving into a much beloved or firmly established custom. You will need not only undisputed evidence but also justifiable cause to challenge some protected *powers that be* particular to your setting. Stephanie L. Dodman and colleagues (2019) find that educator engagement in an equity audit:

> Allows one to collect data related to the many possible inequities within a school and/or classroom in terms of race, class, gender, (dis) ability, sexual identity, language, and so on. Data sources typically include achievement data (e.g., test scores, dropout rates), discipline data (e.g., expulsions, office referrals), tracking data (e.g., identified participants for gifted and special education programs), extracurricular data (e.g., participation rates in athletics and the arts), staffing (e.g., staff diversity and retention), and so on. . . . The educator then selects one area to further examine, determines whether a pattern of inequity is occurring, analyzes the potential causes, collaboratively works to devise a solution, implements the solution, and monitors the results (Scheurich & Skrla, 2003). (pp. 7–8)

The Mid-Atlantic Equity Consortium (MAEC; 2021) published an extensive equity audit tool that covers a range of interrogative evaluation criteria within three major areas: criteria for an equitable school, an equitable classroom, and teacher behaviors. The introduction to the framework alerts us to the following:

> The Equity Audit is a tool that provides a snapshot of your district/ school's state at one point in time. By no means is it exhaustive and does not include all potential systemic barriers to equity or focuses on all groups that might not be receiving required supports. (MAEC, 2021, p. 2)

Within each category are several subheadings that address distinct areas for inquiry. You can use the entire guide for a complete systemwide audit or select the applicable items to appraise individual initiatives you've identified as candidates for review. MAEC's comprehensive audit tool can be accessed at (maec.org /equity-audit). Figure 6.5 summarizes the table of contents and subtopics the tool contains.

Criteria for an Equitable School	Criteria for an Equitable Classroom	Teacher Behaviors
School Policy Assessing Community Needs School Organization and Administration School Climate and Environment Staff Assessment and Placement Professional Learning Standards and Curriculum Development	Academic Placement and Tracking and Grouping Student Leadership and Recognition Classroom Environment Instructional Strategies	Instructional Strategies Curriculum Strategies Classroom Management Techniques Interpersonal Balance Teacher Behaviors That Encourage Student Persistence

Source: MAEC, 2021, p. 3.

Figure 6.5: Table of contents for the MAEC audit tool.

Returning to the two examples in figure 6.4 (page 167), one might select different question stems or prompts that fit each scenario. For instance, in the case of replacing the existing canon of core novels with more culturally responsive texts, the following questions from the sections on Standards and Curriculum Development and Curriculum Strategies are appropriate considerations (MAEC, 2021).

1. "Are all teachers involved in improving the curriculum through continuous and systematized feedback and revision, so that all students can learn and achieve at high levels?" (p. 19)

2. "Are all families and students encouraged to provide feedback on educational programs, both planning and instructional?" (p. 19)

3. "Do recommended textbooks and other instructional materials reflect, as much as possible, the experiences and perspectives of diversity among racial, ethnic, socioeconomic, national origin, language, sexual, gender identity and expression, religious, sexual orientation, or disability status groups?" (p. 19)

4. "Are teachers encouraged to use and provide examples produced by people of different races, ethnicities, socioeconomic statuses, national origins, languages, sexes, gender identities and expressions, sexual orientations, religions, or disability statuses as part of the curriculum?" (p. 20)

5. "[Do they] use culturally responsive pedagogy, practice, and instructional materials that reflect diversity?" (p. 32)

For the second practice described in figure 6.4 (page 167), in which teachers restrict student access to recess, breaks, and lunch as a punishment for minor classroom infractions (talking out of turn, being off task, disrupting others, getting up without permission, not completing classwork, and so on), this set of prompts from the School Policy, School Organization and Administration, and Classroom Management Techniques sections may be illuminating (MAEC, 2021).

1. "Are there policies and procedures to assure that no student is denied participation in extracurricular or co-curricular activities (as health and safety guidelines permit) because of race, ethnicity, socioeconomic status, national origin, English Learner status, sex, gender identity, gender expression, sexual orientation, religion, disability status, or transportation limitations?" (p. 6)

2. "Is data regularly collected, disaggregated, and analyzed . . . by different racial, ethnic, and language groups regarding student discipline, suspensions, and expulsions?" (p. 10)

3. "Are consequences for violating school procedures taught and reinforced to students using evidence-based strategies (e.g., restorative practices, culturally responsive PBIS, etc.)?" (p. 11)

4. "[Does it] demonstrate flexibility, fairness, and compassion in situations which lead to conflict and potential in-person and virtual classroom disruption?" (p. 33)

5. "[Does it] make efforts to address disruptive student behaviors privately in order to support individual growth and positive behavior?" (p. 33)

Once you have completed the audit process, you will make a recommendation similar to the process described in stage 7 if the results of your examination urge some action for change. Whether you decide to approach the initiatives one by one or do a whole system overhaul, take your time to get it right; otherwise, new initiatives may end up as collateral damage and lead to bitterness or resentment.

CONCLUSION

The physical, psychological, and institutional barriers to progress may rear their ugly heads from time to time, but they are dragons worth slaying in the name of equity. I contend that when all is said and done, even resisters will feel some semblance of relief as the organization streamlines and reduces the sheer number of implementations in the system. Instead of futilely trying to balance five competing variations on the same theme, educators will find through this process that they are now responsible for well-designed, purposefully intended, clearly communicated, and efficaciously launched equity-centered initiatives, each at the right pace and time.

Equity-Focused Initiative Assessment Tool

Directions: The guiding questions are linked to the point values assigned to each item in assessing how close the program, product, or service is to meeting school or district equity-centered goals. For ease of phrasing, the generic term *implementation* will be used but is meant to be replaced with more specific descriptors such as *master scheduling, physical education standards, robotics program, SEL curriculum, zero waste project,* and so on. Rate each criterion to arrive at a total score.

Implementation: [Add details here]

Guiding Questions	Rating Scale (low to high)				
1. Is the implementation, as it stands, strategically aligned to the most recent versions of equity-centered district plans?	1	2	3	4	5
2. Is the implementation making a direct and measurable impact on the intended student groups?	1	2	3	4	5
3. Has the implementation helped to close performance gaps between identified student groups?	1	2	3	4	5
4. How well does the implementation connect to or advance other concurrent equity-centered initiatives?	1	2	3	4	5
5. Does the implementation have support from the students, families, and staff it is meant to serve?	1	2	3	4	5
6. Is the implementation still relevant and meaningful for 21st century learning and diverse postsecondary college and career readiness?	1	2	3	4	5
7. Do the contributions to educational equity justify the level of investment or resources to keep it up to date?	1	2	3	4	5
8. Is the implementation (still) required by law or moral obligation to marginalized students?	1	2	3	4	5
9. Do we have a superior implementation to fill its prior role in the organization?	1	2	3	4	5
10. If eliminated, how intense would the opposition to its removal be by minority groups who might retain benefits from it?	1	2	3	4	5
Scoring Guide:	Total:				

Scoring Guide:

10–24 points: Eliminate the implementation.

25–39 points: Conduct more outreach and reevaluate.

40–50 points: Keep the implementation.

Source: Adapted from Wallace, K. (2022). Leading the launch: A ten-stage process for successful district initiatives. Bloomington, IN: Solution Tree Press.

Cost-Impact Matrix

Directions: Before you begin to fill out the matrix, you'll need to gather a minimum of two data points for each initiative you plan to deconstruct: (1) *total costs* including staffing, resources, materials, training, salaries, and so on, and (2) *valid data* to show progress, achievement, or targeted outcomes met by identified groups of historically underserved students in your schools. Then your team will come to consensus before listing each initiative in the most appropriate box. The items that land in low impact quadrants (1 and 2) are candidates for elimination during the next part of the retirement process.

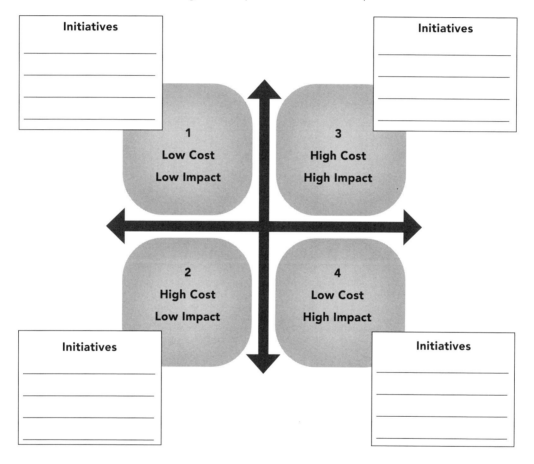

Source: Wallace, K. (2022). Leading the launch: A ten-stage process for successful district initiatives. Bloomington, IN: Solution Tree Press.

Implementation Inspection

Existing Initiative Implementation	Cost-to-Impact Ratio	Opportunities for Inclusion and Equity Focus	Recommendation to Superintendent or Governing Body
			☐ Keep as is. ☐ Revise for inclusion and equity. ☐ Propose retirement
			☐ Keep as is. ☐ Revise for inclusion and equity. ☐ Propose retirement.
			☐ Keep as is. ☐ Revise for inclusion and equity. ☐ Propose retirement.

Vetting for Equity in Legacy Practices

Directions: Circle prepopulated items or add your own specific examples in the left column regarding legacy practices or inherited implementations in your organization. Then answer the questions in the right column to determine whether they are still efficacious relation to the student groups you've identified to close opportunity gaps.

Long-Term Educational Practices	Vetting for Educational Equity Efficacy
Instructional (Circle any that apply): Homework, test prep, copying down lecture notes, rote memorization, filling in worksheets, repetition **Additional Practices to Examine:**	Is the instructional practice still benefiting diverse groups of students? How do you know? Is the practice supported by progressive and conclusive educational research? Will the practice help develop college and career skills and key competencies that marginalized students will need for their postsecondary future?
Assessment (Circle any that apply): Pop quizzes, weighted grades, zeros for not completing assignments, red ink, standardized testing, report cards, A–F grading **Additional Practices to Examine:**	Does the practice motivate all students to improve or discourage some non-dominant groups' progress? Has the practice disproportionately negatively impacted specific demographics of students? If so, which groups and why? Is the practice a realistic, reliable, and valid means of assessing what students know and can do? Does it favor certain groups over others?

continued ▶

Leading Through an Equity Lens © 2023 Solution Tree Press • SolutionTree.com
Visit **go.SolutionTree.com/diversityandequity** to download this page.

Long-Term Educational Practices	Vetting for Educational Equity Efficacy
Disciplinary (Circle any that apply): Suspensions for truancy, recess detention, dress codes or school uniforms, zero tolerance for drugs or violence, cell phone bans, Saturday school	Do the data show discrepancies in application of the policy to different students by race, gender, language, socioeconomics, special needs, or cultural background? Describe how.
Additional Practices to Examine:	Does the practice inspire behavioral changes or increased self-discipline equivalently among and between all student groups?
	Are the practices the best alternatives the school can use to improve school climate, culture, and safety? Including for historically disenfranchised students?
Organizational (Circle any that apply): Bell schedules, busing, hall passes, bathroom permissions, school start and end times, desks in rows	Is there a solid rationale and explanation for the practice? Does the mechanism still function reasonably well for today's students from all backgrounds?
Additional Practices to Examine:	Do students across the district experience the same benefits (or penalties) of the practice?
	Does the practice affect different segments of the school population fairly? Does it work?

continued ▲

page 2 of 3

Long-Term Educational Practices	Vetting for Educational Equity Efficacy
Traditions (Circle any that apply): Science fairs, spelling bees, talent contests, pep rallies, assemblies, school rivalries, homecoming court **Additional Practices to Examine:**	Is the practice primarily a White, heteronormative legacy that lacks relevance to non-White, non-straight pupils? How do students of color, racial minorities, linguistically diverse, and LGBTQ+ students tend to fare in these competitions? Does the practice encourage unity or create greater divisions between student groups?
Stratification (Circle any that apply): Ability grouping; academic (basic, college prep, honors) and vocational tracking; retention for failure; gifted and talented education; special education; language, racial, and social inequities; class rankings **Additional Practices to Examine:**	When disaggregating the data, are minoritized students equitably represented in the advanced learning environments or relegated to lower-track paths? Is the practice necessary to comply with higher education admission criteria or workplace employment or are there alternative measures that can be leveraged instead? What are the short- and long-term effects or consequences of maintaining the practice on marginalized students?

Epilogue

This epilogue might be more aptly titled *prologue*. Throughout this book, we've dug up the past, delved into the present, and designed for a better future. Well, the future is here. *You created it*. Seriously. You've literally altered what the students who walk through your schools' doors will experience by generating implementations that work, that are high functioning, and that persist and prevail. Those positive impacts will change not only the trajectories of individual students' lives but benefit society as well. Let's peek into the not-so-distant future to confirm that our efforts to advance equity are heading in the right direction.

A 2018 press release from the U.S. Census Bureau correctly projected that 2020 would become the year that fewer than half of the children born in the United States would be non-Hispanic Whites. The report also predicted that by 2045, those children's elders would reach minority status of just under 49 percent. Since 1964, the NCES has also been projecting education trends for schools in the United States. The NCES projects statistics up through the year 2028 (as cited in Hussar & Bailey, 2020). In general, public school enrollment is projected to increase 2 percent to 51.4 million, and private school enrollment to increase by 3 percent to 6 million between 2016 and 2028 (as cited in Hussar & Bailey, 2020). The racial enrollment in public elementary and secondary schools is projected to (as cited in Hussar & Bailey, 2020):

- decrease 7 percent between 2016 and 2028 for students who are White;
- increase 1 percent between 2016 and 2028 for students who are Black;
- increase 8 percent between 2016 and 2028 for students who are Hispanic;

· increase 20 percent between 2016 and 2028 for students who
  are Asian/Pacific Islander;

· decrease 7 percent between 2016 and 2028 for students who
  are American Indian/Alaska Native; and

· increase 51 percent between 2016 and 2028 for students who
  are of Two or more races (p. 7)

While the fluctuations in different parts of the country may not exactly reflect these demographic breakdowns, the overall portrait of the United States is one of increasing racial and ethnic diversity. It's not a melting pot or salad bowl but an exquisite feast. What does this mean for educators? *Now is already here* for the millions of young people in our schools who need us to teach them differently, reach them through cultural awareness, and lead with them at the center.

This book started with a rather grim view of education but ends with hope. We don't have to continue doing the same things over and over, expecting different results. Early educational philosopher John Dewey's (1944) words are timeless and still an aspiration (though whether or not he actually said them as attributed is nebulous): "If we teach today's students as we taught yesterday's, we rob them of tomorrow."

So just imagine what the future may hold as a result of equity-centered initiatives in your school district.

- Improved academic, social-emotional, and developmental outcomes for historically marginalized students

- An equity-centered protocol that all leaders in your organization collectively subscribe to and follow

- Elimination of unproductive or harmful practices that impede progress

- Increased engagement and satisfaction from all stakeholders

- Reduced waste of resources including time, money, effort, morale, capital expenditures, materials, and staffing

- Transformation of school culture to one of greater diversity, inclusion, and belonging

- Increased respect, understanding, and expectations for minoritized student groups in your community

- Clarity, cohesion, precision, and competence!

Hopefully, this book has given you a set of research-based practical applications to help you begin to work toward your equity goals. Use the "Equity-Centered Initiatives Checklist" reproducible on page 182 as a final check to assure that your equity-centered initiatives are ready for launch.

We are the system. The system is us. Once we acknowledge the false paradigm that we are separate beings, we can enact purposeful change. Ontologically speaking, the individual and professional decisions we make affect the whole. By both harnessing and respecting that power, leaders can make permanent imprints on the field for decades to come. You may not see the immediate impacts or know what your thousands of colleagues across the globe are doing in complement to your efforts, but know that your community is out there.

When I was a senior in high school, I asked a teacher of mine how she stayed so invested in the Amnesty International human rights work she was so devoted to, in the face of never really knowing whether her personal involvement made a difference. She said something to the effect of, *what truly matters is that we each pick our little corner of the world to sweep*. That image has stuck with me ever since, and whenever I feel overwhelmed with the gravity of being an educator, I pick up my metaphorical broom and get back to sweeping my own little *umwelt* in the hope that it crosses paths someday with yours.

This lesser-known Dewey (1938) quote from *Experience and Education* muses:

> We always live at the time we live and not at some other time, and only by extracting at each present time the full meaning of each present experience are we prepared for doing the same thing in the future. (p. 49)

Everything you have gained and applied from reading this book will inhabit both your own mind and the next generation of minds you inspire. And therein lies the magic.

Equity-Centered Initiatives Checklist

Chapters	Action Planning	Notes or Evidence
Introduction	☐ *Review* Leading the Launch: A Ten-Stage Process for Successful District Initiatives *for orientation (Wallace, 2022).* ☐ *Determine which student groups in your school or district would benefit most from equity-centered initiatives.*	
Chapter 1: Barriers to Equity	☐ *Discuss questions for consideration for first-, second-, and third-order barriers with your team. (Reproducibles on pages 25, 26, and 27).* ☐ *Engage in an initiative autopsy exercise in figure 1.1 (page 20).* ☐ *Examine district dynamics in figure 1.2 (page 23).*	
Chapter 2: Initial Stages	☐ *Define your most pressing equity-centered problems of practice in figure 2.1 (page 33) and table 2.1 (page 35).* ☐ *Get ready for stage 1 by winding up the pitch in figure 2.2 (page 38).* ☐ *Conduct your tuning protocol in figure 2.3 (page 41).* ☐ *Complete stage 2 with the post pitch SWOT analysis in figure 2.4 (page 43).* ☐ *Prioritize your initiatives in stage 3 using the weighted rubric in figure 2.8 (page 50).*	

Chapters	Action Planning	Notes or Evidence
Chapter 3: Trial Stages	☐ *Respond to the feasibility measures prompts in figure 3.1 (page 67).* ☐ *Use the stage 4 pilot planning template in figure 3.2 (page 69) to prep your experiment.* ☐ *Work on engagement in stage 5 using table 3.1 (page 75) and figure 3.3 (page 77).* ☐ *Map out your community using the guidelines in stage 6 (page 83).*	
Chapter 4: Decision-Making Stage	☐ *Apply the evaluation to your proposed initiative using figure 4.1 (page 102).* ☐ *Research your organization's governance structure and approval processes using figure 4.2 (page 104).* ☐ *Fill out your stage 7 school board memo template in figure 4.5 (page 111).* ☐ *Draft your stage 7 request for school board approval in figure 4.7 (page 112).*	
Chapter 5: Execution Stages	☐ *Explore staff mentalities in stage 8 using the iceberg model in figure 5.3 (page 127).* ☐ *Develop your own SMARTIE goals in figure 5.4 (page 132).* ☐ *Take inventory of your existing initiatives in stage 9 using figure 5.5 (page 135).* ☐ *Fill out your own stage 10 annual planning calendar in figure 5.6 (page 143).*	

Chapters	Action Planning	Notes or Evidence
Chapter 6: Making Space	☐ Evaluate individual programs using the equity-focused initiative assessment tool in figure 6.1 (page 155). ☐ Analyze major district initiatives with the cost-to-impact ratios in figure 6.2 (page 161). ☐ Closely inspect your legacy implementations for efficacy with figure 6.4 (page 167). ☐ Check out the MAEC audit tool used in figure 6.5 (page 169)	
Epilogue	☐ Imagine the results of executing equity-centered initiatives in your school district. ☐ Pick your own little corner of the world to sweep.	

References and Resources

Allen, D. (1995). *The tuning protocol: A process for reflection.* (Studies on Exhibitions, No. 15). Providence, RI: Coalition of Essential Schools, Brown University.

Andrews, D. J. C., & Richmond, G. (2019). Professional development for equity: What constitutes powerful professional learning? *Journal of Teacher Education, 70*(5), 408–409.

Askell-Williams, H., & Koh, G. A. (2020). Enhancing the sustainability of school improvement initiatives. *School Effectiveness and School Improvement, 31*(4), 660–678.

Bada, F. (2020, January 23). *Countries with the highest high school graduate rates.* Accessed at worldatlas.com/articles/countries-with-the-highest-high-school-graduate-rates.html on November 3, 2022.

Bailey, K., & Jakicic, C. (2012). *Common formative assessment: A toolkit for Professional Learning Communities at Work.* Bloomington, IN: Solution Tree Press.

Benzaghta, M. A., Elwalda, A., Mousa, M. M., Erkan, I., & Rahman, M. (2021). SWOT analysis applications: An integrative literature review. *Journal of Global Business Insights, 6*(1), 55–73.

Brown v. Board of Education of Topeka, 347 U.S. 483 (1954).

Bueno-Guerra N. (2018). How to apply the concept of umwelt in the evolutionary study of cognition. *Frontiers in Psychology, 9*(2001).

Burns, T. (2017). Neurodiversity in education. *Trends Shaping Education Spotlight, 12.* Accessed at https://www.academia.edu/34893736/Neurodiversity_in_Education_Neuro developmental_diversity_the_cases_of_Autism_and_ADHD on February 17, 2023.

Capper, C. A., & Young, M. D. (2015). The equity audit as the core of leading increasingly diverse schools and districts. In G. Theoharis & M. Scanlan (Eds.), *Leadership for increasingly diverse schools* (pp. 186–197). New York: Routledge.

Carnegie Project on the Education Doctorate. (n.d.). *The CPED Framework.* Accessed at cpedinitiative.org/the-framework on November 2, 2022.

Center for Creative Leadership. (2020, November 23). *10 steps for establishing team norms.* Accessed at ccl.org/articles/leading-effectively-articles/the-real-world-guide-to-team-norms on December 30, 2022.

Center for Mental Health in Schools at UCLA. (n.d.). *Mapping existing school and community resources for addressing barriers to learning.* Accessed at smhp.psych.ucla.edu/qf/p2312_06.htm on January 4, 2023.

Chiefs for Change. (2022, August). *The implementation engine: A guidebook to support leaders from initiative planning to execution.* Washington, DC: Authors. Accessed at chiefsforchange .org/download-media/the-implementation-engine-a-guidebook-to-support-leaders-from -initiative-planning-to-execution on November 2, 2022.

Civil Rights Act of 1964, Pub. L. No. 88-352, 78 Stat. 241 (1964).

Collaborative for Academic, Social, and Emotional Learning. (2020). *Develop goals for schoolwide SEL.* Accessed at https://schoolguide.casel.org/resource/developing-goals-for -schoolwide-sel on January 9, 2023.

Conzemius, A. E., & O'Neill, J. (2014). *The handbook for SMART school teams: Revitalizing best practices for collaboration* (2nd ed.). Bloomington, IN: Solution Tree Press.

Coronavirus Aid, Relief, and Economic Security Act (CARES Act), Pub. L. 116–136 (2020).

Cristofaro, M. (2017). Reducing biases of decision-making processes in complex organizations. *Management Research Review, 40*(3), 270–291.

Davis, B. (2021, December 6). *Holding students back—An inequitable and ineffective response to unfinished learning.* Accessed at https://edtrust.org/resource/holding-students-back-an -inequitable-and-ineffective-response-to-unfinished-learning/ on January 3, 2023.

Deming, W. E. (2000). *Out of the crisis.* Cambridge, MA: MIT Press.

Dewey, J. (1938). *Experience and education.* New York: Macmillan.

Dewey, J. (1944). *Democracy and education: An introduction to the philosophy of education.* New York: Free Press.

Digital Promise. (2019). *Asset mapping: A guide for educational innovation cluster.* Washington, DC: Author. Accessed at digitalpromise.org/wp-content/uploads/2018/09/asset -mapping.pdf on January 4, 2023.

Dodman, S. L., DeMulder, E. K., View, J. L., Swalwell, K., Stribling, S., Ra, S., et al. (2019). Equity audits as a tool of critical data-driven decision making: Preparing teachers to see beyond achievement gaps and bubbles. *Action in Teacher Education, 41*(1), 4–22.

Doran, G. T. (1981). There's a S.M.A.R.T. way to write management's goals and objectives. *Management Review, 70*(11), 35–36.

Dryden-Peterson, S. (2019). Refugee education: Backward design to enable futures. *Education and Conflict Review, 2,* 49–53. Accessed at discovery.ucl.ac.uk/id/eprint/10081586/1/Dryden -Peterson_Article_08_Dryden-Peterson.pdf on January 5, 2023.

Dryden-Peterson, S., Adelman, E., Bellino, M. J., & Chopra, V. (2019). The purposes of refugee education: Policy and practice of including refugees in national education systems. *Sociology of Education, 92*(4), 346–366.

DuFour, R., & DuFour, R. (2015). *How effective leaders develop consensus and address resistance* [Slideshow presentation]. Accessed at https://soltreemrls3.s3-us-west -2.amazonaws.com/solution-tree.com/media/pdf/powerpoints/leadership-now-2015/R-R DuFour-HowEffectiveLeadersDevelopConsensus.pdf on December 29, 2022.

Easton, L. B. (2002, March 1). How the tuning protocol works. *ASCD*. Accessed at www.ascd .org/el/articles/how-the-tuning-protocol-works on January 1, 2022.

Education Amendments Act of 1972, 20 U. S. C. §1681–1688 (1972).

Equal Educational Opportunities Act of 1974, 93–380, title II, §201, 88 Stat. 514 (1974).

Feiten, T. E. (2022). Jakob von Uexküll's concept of umwelt. *The Philosopher*, *110*(1). Accessed at thephilosopher1923.org/post/jakob-von-uexkull-umwelt on December 27, 2022.

Feldman, J. (2018). *Grading for equity: What it is, why it matters, and how it can transform schools and classrooms*. Thousand Oaks, CA: Corwin Press.

Filardo, M., Vincent, J. M., & Sullivan, K. (2018). *Education equity requires modern school facilities*. Washington, DC: 21st Century School Fund. Accessed at https://static1.square space.com/static/5a6ca11af9a61e2c7be7423e/t/5ba23b3688251b659c2f9eff/153735867 1343/Education+Equity+Requires+Modern+School+Facilities.pdf on November 2, 2022.

Frontier, T. (2021). *Teaching with clarity: How to prioritize and do less so students understand more*. Alexandria, VA: ASCD.

Gorski, P. (2019, April 19). Avoiding racial equity detours. *ASCD*. Accessed at ascd.org/el /articles/avoiding-racial-equity-detours on November 2, 2022.

Green, E. L. (2023, January 1). Strife in the schools: Education dept. logs record number of discrimination complaints. *The New York Times*. Accessed at www.nytimes.com/2023/01/01 /us/politics/education-discrimination.html on January 1, 2023.

Gregory, J. L. (2017) Trust relationships in schools: Supporting or subverting implementation of school-wide initiatives. *School Leadership and Management*, *37*(1–2), 141–161.

Halbert, J., & Kaser, L. (2022) *Leading through spirals of inquiry: For equity and quality*. Winnipeg, Manitoba, Canada: Portage & Main Press.

Hanson, M. (2022a, July 26). *College enrollment & student demographic statistics*. Accessed at educationdata.org/college-enrollment-statistics on November 2, 2022.

Hanson, M. (2022b, June 15). *U.S. public education spending statistics*. Accessed at https://educationdata.org/public-education-spending-statistics#:~:text=Report%20 Highlights.,fund%20K%2D12%20public%20education on November 2, 2022.

Hargreaves, A., & Fink, D. (2006). *Sustainable leadership*. San Francisco: Jossey-Bass.

Hargraves, V. (2019, April 8). How to build partnerships with families from different cultural backgrounds. *The Education Hub*. Accessed at theeducationhub.org.nz/how-to-build -partnerships-with-families-from-different-cultural-backgrounds on January 3, 2023.

Hegewisch, A., & Mariano, H. (2020, September 16). *Same gap, different year: The gender wage gap, 2019 earnings differences by gender, race, and ethnicity*. Accessed at iwpr.org/iwpr-issues /esme/same-gap-different-year-the-gender-wage-gap-2019-earnings-differences-by-gender -race-and-ethnicity on November 3, 2022.

Hess, F. M., & Wright, B. L. (Eds.). (2020). *Getting the most bang for the education buck.* New York: Teachers College Press.

Hollister, R., & Watkins, M. D. (2018). Too many projects: How to deal with initiative overload. *Harvard Business Review.* Accessed at https://hbr.org/2018/09/too-many-projects on November 2, 2022.

hooks, b. (1994). *Teaching to transgress: Education as the practice of freedom.* London: Routledge.

Hussar, W. J., & Bailey, T. M. (2020). *Projections of education statistics to 2028.* Washington, DC: National Center for Education Statistics.

International Commission on the Futures of Education. (2021). *Reimagining our futures together: A new social contract for education.* Paris, France: United Nations Educational, Scientific and Cultural Organization (UNESCO). Accessed at reliefweb.int/report/world /reimagining-our-futures-together-new-social-contract-education on January 6, 2023.

Jackson, J., & McIver, M. (n.d.). *Using equity-centered capacity building to advance school system improvement.* Accessed at capacitybuildingnetwork.org/article2 on November 2, 2022.

Jurado de Los Santos, P., Moreno-Guerrero, A. J., Marín-Marín, J. A., & Soler Costa, R. (2020). The term equity in education: A literature review with scientific mapping in web of science. *International Journal of Environmental Research and Public Health, 17*(10), 3526.

Kober, N., & Rentner, D. S. (2020). *History and evolution of public education in the US.* Washington, DC: Center on Education Policy at The George Washington University.

Ladson-Billings, G. (2021) Three decades of culturally relevant, responsive, & sustaining pedagogy: What lies ahead? *The Educational Forum, 85*(4), 351–354.

Langley, G. J., Moen, R. D., Nolan, K. M., Nolan, T. W., Norman, C. L., & Provost, L. P. (2009). *The improvement guide: A practical approach to enhancing organizational performance* (2nd ed.). San Francisco: Jossey-Bass.

Levinson, M., Geron, T., & Brighouse, H. (2022). Conceptions of educational equity. *AERA Open,* 8.

Locke, J., Lee, K., Cook, C. R., Frederick, L., Vázques-Colón, C., Ehrhart, M. G., et al. (2019). Understanding the organizational implementation context of schools: A qualitative study of school district administrators, principals, and teachers. *School Mental Health, 11,* 379–399.

Maslow, A. H. (1943). A theory of human motivation. *Psychological Review, 50*(4), 370–396.

Maslow, A. H. (1954). *Motivation and personality.* New York: Harper & Row.

Mathewson, T. G. (2020, October 31). New data: Even within the same district some wealthy schools get millions more than poor ones. *The Hechinger Report.* Accessed at hechingerreport .org/new-data-even-within-the-same-district-some-wealthy-schools-get-millions-more-than -poor-ones on August 6, 2022.

Mid-Atlantic Equity Consortium. (2021). *MAEC's equity audit.* Accessed at maec.org/equity -audit on November 2, 2022.

Moen, R., & Norman, C. (2009, September 17). *The history of the PDCA cycle* [Conference presentation]. Seventh Asian Network for Quality Congress, Tokyo, Japan.

Moreno, K., & Song, X. (2021). Intentional stakeholder engagement that fosters innovation and equity. *Intersection: A Journal at the Intersection of Assessment and Learning, 2*(3).

Murphy, M. (2015, June 25). In change management, start with champions, not antagonists. *Forbes.* Accessed at forbes.com/sites/markmurphy/2015/06/25/in-change-management-start -with-champions-not-antagonists/?sh=d9bc95cbd0a9 on December 27, 2022.

National Center for Complementary and Integrative Health. (n.d.). *Pilot studies: Common uses and misuses.* Accessed at nccih.nih.gov/grants/pilot-studies-common-uses-and-misuses on December 31, 2022.

National Center for Education Statistics. (2022, May). *Public school expenditures.* Accessed at https://nces.ed.gov/programs/coe/indicator/cmb on November 3, 2022.

National School Boards Association. (2018). *Today's school boards & their priorities for tomorrow.* Accessed at cdn-files.nsba.org/s3fs-public/reports/K12_National_Survey.pdf on January 5, 2023.

Neumann, J. W. (2018). How power really works in schools. *Phi Delta Kappan, 99*(8), 30–35.

Nomensen, T. (2018). *Teacher talk: How many White, middle class, female educators perpetuate White privilege in school.* [Doctoral dissertation, University of Missouri-St. Louis.] Institutional Respository Library. https://irl.umsl.edu/dissertation/770

Noor Ismail, S., Muhammad, S., Omar, M. N., & Raman, A. (2020). The great challenge of Malaysian school leaders' instructional leadership: Can it affect teachers' functional competency across 21st century education? *Universal Journal of Educational Research, 8*(6), 2436–2443.

Organisation for Economic Co-operation and Development. (2008, January). *Ten steps to equity in education.* Paris: OECD Publishing. Accessed at oecd.org/education/school/39989494.pdf on November 3, 2022.

Organisation for Economic Co-operation and Development. (2016). *Trends shaping education 2016.* Paris: Author.

Organisation for Economic Co-operation and Development. (2017). *Trends shaping education spotlight 12.* Paris: Author. Accessed at oecd.org/education/ceri/Spotlight12 -Neurodiversity.pdf on November 2, 2022.

Pfeffer, J., & Sutton, R. I. (2000). *The knowing-doing gap: How smart companies turn knowledge into action.* Boston: Harvard Business School Press.

Poekert, P. E., Swaffield, S., Demir, E. K., & Wright, S. A. (2020) Leadership for professional learning towards educational equity: A systematic literature review. *Professional Development in Education, 46*(4), 541–562.

Regional Educational Laboratory Appalachia at SRI International. (2021, May). *Learning before going to scale: An introduction to conducting pilot studies.* Washington, DC: Institute of Education Sciences. Accessed at https://ies.ed.gov/ncee/edlabs/regions/appalachia/resources /pdfs/Pilot-Study-Resource_acc.pdf on November 2, 2022.

Reich, J. (2022, October 1). *The power of doing less in schools.* Accessed at ascd.org/el/articles /the-power-of-doing-less-in-schools on November 3, 2022.

Reid, K. (2023, January 25). *What is a refugee?* Accessed at worldvision.org/refugees-news -stories/what-is-a-refugee-facts on January 6, 2023.

Reimers, F. M. (Ed.) (2022). *Primary and secondary education during Covid-19: Disruptions to educational opportunity during a pandemic.* Cham, Switzerland: Springer Open Access.

Rick, T. (2014). Organizational culture is like an iceberg [Blog post]. Accessed at https://torben rick.eu/blog/culture/organizational-culture-is-like-an-iceberg/amp on November 3, 2022.

Riordan, M., Klein, E. J., & Gaynor, C. (2019) Teaching for equity and deeper learning: How does professional learning transfer to teachers' practice and influence students' experiences? *Equity & Excellence in Education, 52*(2–3), 327–345.

Robinson, K. J. (2021, December 27). *Protecting education as a civil right: Remedying racial discrimination and ensuring a high-quality education.* Palo Alto, CA: Learning Policy Institute.

Rushton, S., Morgan, J., & Richard, M. (2007). Teacher's Myers-Briggs personality profiles: Identifying effective teacher personality traits. *Teaching and Teacher Education, 23*(4), 432–441.

Ryan, R. M., & Deci, E. L. (2000). Self-determination theory and the facilitation of intrinsic motivation, social development, and well-being. *American Psychologist, 55*(1), 68–78. Accessed at https://selfdeterminationtheory.org/SDT/documents/2000_RyanDeci_SDT.pdf on April 7, 2023.

Sainio, M., Herkama, S., Turunen, T., Rönkkö, M., Kontio, M., Poskiparta, E., et al. (2020). Sustainable antibullying program implementation: School profiles and predictors. *Scandinavian Journal of Psychology, 61*(1), 132–142.

Samuels, P. (2020, April). *A really simple guide to quantitative data analysis.* Accessed at www.researchgate.net/publication/340838762_A_Really_Simple_Guide_to_Quantitative _Data_Analysis?channel=doi&linkId=5ea03d3f92851cee1a2b95a5&showFulltext=true on January 31, 2023.

Scheurich, J. J., & Skrla, L. (2003). *Leadership for equity and excellence: Creating high-achievement classrooms, schools, and districts.* Thousand Oaks, CA: Corwin Press.

Schmoker, M. (2004). Learning communities at the crossroads: Toward the best schools we've ever had. *The Phi Delta Kappan, 86*(1), 84–88.

Schnellert, L. (Ed.). (2020). *Professional learning networks: Facilitating transformation in diverse contexts with equity-seeking communities.* Bingley, England: Emerald.

Senge, P. (2006) *The fifth discipline: The art and practice of the learning organization.* New York: Doubleday.

Shields, L., Newman, A., & Satz, D. (2017, May 31). Equality of educational opportunity. In E. N. Zalta (Ed.), *The Stanford Encyclopedia of Philosophy.* Accessed at plato.stanford.edu /archives/sum2017/entries/equal-ed-opportunity on November 3, 2022.

Skerrett, A., Warrington, A., & Williamson, T. (2018). *Generative principles for professional learning for equity-oriented urban English teachers.* Washington, DC: National Council of Teachers of English. Accessed at https://lead.nwp.org/wp-content/uploads/2020/06 /AllisonSkerrett-GenerativePrinciples.pdf on January 31, 2023.

Strunk, K. K., & Locke, L. A. (Eds.). (2019). *Research methods for social justice and equity in education.* London: Palgrave Macmillan.

Swerdlow, D. (2019, January 14). *What's better than SMART goals? Try SMARTIE goals* [Blog post]. Accessed at idealist.org/en/careers/better-than-smart-smartie-goals on November 3, 2022.

Thattai, D. (2001). *A history of public education in the United States.* Accessed at academia.edu /5177440/A_history_of_public_education_in_the_United_States on November 3, 2022.

Tichnor-Wagner, A., Allen, D., Socol, A. R., Cohen-Vogel, L., Rutledge, S. A., & Xing, Q. W. (2018). Studying implementation within a continuous-improvement process: What happens when we design with adaptations in mind? *Teachers College Record, 120*(5), 1–52.

United Nations Educational, Scientific, and Cultural Organization (UNESCO) Institute for Statistics. (2022). *Government expenditure per student, secondary (% of GDP per capita).* Accessed at data.worldbank.org/indicator/SE.XPD.SECO.PC.ZS on April 3, 2022.

United Nations High Commissioner for Refugees. (2022). *Global trends: Forced displacement in 2021.* Copenhagen, Denmark: Author. Accessed at unhcr.org/62a9d1494/global-trends -report-2021 on January 6, 2023.

United States Census Bureau (2018, March 13). *Older people projected to outnumber children for first time in U.S. history* [Press release]. Accessed at census.gov/newsroom/press-releases /2018/cb18-41-population-projections.html on November 3, 2022.

United States Census Bureau. (2022, May). *Detailed occupation by sex education age earnings: ACS 2019.* Accessed at census.gov/data/tables/2022/demo/acs-2019.html on November 2, 2022.

USA Facts. (2020, December 4). Who are the nation's 4 million teachers? Accessed at https:// usafacts.org/articles/who-are-the-nations-4m-teachers on December 27, 2022.

von Uexküll, J. (2010). *A foray into the worlds of animals and humans: With a theory of meaning.* Minneapolis, MN: University of Minnesota Press.

Wallace, K. (2012). *Teachers and technology: Identifying uses, barriers, and strategies to support classroom integration* [Doctoral dissertation, University of California, Davis]. ProQuest Dissertations. proquest.com/openview/63cba9453b1c78cbb6aaf60456eaa077/1 ?pq-origsite=gscholar&cbl=18750

Wallace, K. (2022). *Leading the launch: A ten-stage process for successful district initiatives.* Bloomington, IN: Solution Tree Press.

Wang, Y. (2019). Is data-driven decision making at odds with moral decision making? A critical review of school leaders' decision making in the era of school accountability. *Values and Ethics in Educational Administration, 14*(2), 1–9.

Washburn, M. (2020, December 8). *Change management 101: How knowing your stakeholders can make or break your project.* Accessed at cohencpa.com/knowledge-center/insights /ecember-2020/change-management-101-how-knowing-your-stakeholders-can-make-or -break-your-project on January 3, 2023.

Wiggins, G., & McTighe, J. (2005). *Understanding by Design* (2nd ed.). Alexandria, VA: ASCD.

Wilson, V. (2020, June 22). *Inequities exposed: How COVID-19 widened racial inequities in education, health, and the workforce. Testimony before the U.S. House of Representatives Committee on Education and Labor.* Accessed at epi.org/publication/covid-19-inequities-wilson-testimony on January 7, 2023.

World Economic Forum. (2021, March). *Global gender gap report 2021.* Cologny, Switzerland: Author. Accessed at www3.weforum.org/docs/WEF_GGGR_2021.pdf on December 27, 2022.

Yeats, W. B. (2008) The second coming. In R. DiYanni.(Ed.), *Literature: Reading fiction, poetry, and drama* (pp. 188–201). New York: McGraw-Hill. (Original work published 1919)

Zoukis, C. (2017, May 11). Basic literacy: A crucial tool to stem school to prison pipeline. *Huffpost.* Accessed at www.huffpost.com/entry/basic-literacy-a-crucial-tool-to-stem-school-to-prison_b_59149393e4b01ad573dac1dd on February 1, 2023.

Index

Leading the Launch
Kim Wallace
How do schools and districts make true progress?
One step at a time. *Leading the Launch* offers a ten-stage
initiative implementation process proven to help you lead the
charge for change with ingenuity, flexibility, responsiveness,
and passion.
BKG030

Evident Equity
Lauryn Mascareñaz
Make equity the norm in your school or district. *Evident
Equity* provides a comprehensive method that leaders can use
to integrate equitable practices into every facet of their school
communities and offers real-life examples at the elementary,
middle, and high school levels.
BKG032

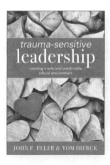

Trauma-Sensitive Leadership
John F. Eller and Tom Hierck
Lead a foundational shift in the way your school approaches
student behavior. Using straightforward language, the
authors offer research-based, practical strategies for
understanding and supporting trauma-impacted students
and providing a safe environment for them to learn.
BKF911

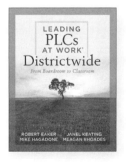

Leading PLCs at Work® Districtwide
Robert Eaker, Mike Hagadone, Janel Keating, and Meagan Rhoades
Ensure your district is doing the right work, the right way, for
the right reasons. With this resource as your guide, you will
learn how to align the work of every PLC team districtwide—
from the boardroom to the classroom.
BKF942

Solution Tree | Press *a division of*
Solution Tree

Visit SolutionTree.com or call 800.733.6786 to order.

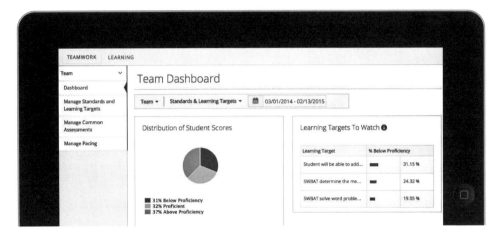